Praise for *Knock! Knock!*

"*Knock! Knock!* is no joke! A fast-paced romp of a read, *Knock! Knock!* — in today's time of branding and selling yourself and what you do — is a must for anyone who needs some sage and hilarious advice. You learn through his excellent storytelling what to do and what not to do to promote whatever you are selling. As someone who has devoted her life to promoting authors, books, literacy, and reading, I know that sometimes we have to get out of our comfort zone, and Doug Thompson tells you how. He has written the definitive guide to being a Sales SUPERSTAR! Five Diamonds in the International Pulpwood Queens Book Club reading mandatory Tiara! Doug deserves to wear the crown for being KING of creating success in business."

— **Kathy L. Murphy,**
CEO and Founder of the International Pulpwood Queens and
Timber Guys Book Club Reading Nation and author of
The Pulpwood Queens' Tiara Wearing, Book Sharing Guide to Life

"A lot of us are accidental salespeople — meaning that we have to learn the skills, attitudes, and techniques necessary for sales success. In *Knock! Knock!* Doug Thompson serves as your professional guide on your positive, fun-filled sales journey. Put Doug's principles to work and you'll be unbeatable."

— **Bryan Flanagan,**
CEO, The Flanagan Training Group and former Director of
Training for Zig Ziglar Corporation, and author of
Now Go Sell Somebody Something!

"This is a must-read book for anyone in the world of sales or thinking about sales. The author doesn't re-hash tired, old topics. Instead, he shares first-hand, personal techniques from his successful sales career spanning several decades. It's like getting the playbook from a winning Super Bowl quarterback. *Knock! Knock!* is a definitive roadmap for your own selling success."

**— Mitchel Whitington,
author and speaker on East Texas history**

"If I were involved in management or training of sales agents, I would make *Knock! Knock!* the top of the list of required reading before beginning a job. I have never been directly involved in sales, per se, but anyone who has any business of any kind and deals with the public, is selling every day.

One's entire life's work, from teaching your children to become good adults, to running your business, involves selling. Doug has done a masterful job of laying out things one must do in order to attain those goals. The author adeptly demonstrated, by telling stories of his successes and failures, that one must believe in oneself, believe in the product you are selling, and enjoy talking about it.

Knock! Knock! is a great instruction manual for anyone in sales, and it also teaches many essential principles of good character. In addition to being instructional, it is also very entertaining. I had a lot of good laughs as I followed the progress of the author's journey through life. I would highly recommend it to anyone, but especially anyone thinking of going into sales."

**— L.C. Dunlop, M.D.
(retired) and author**

KNOCK! KNOCK!

Lessons Learned and Stories Shared

A Ride-Along with
SALES SUPERSTAR
DOUGLAS THOMPSON
with Echo Montgomery Garrett

LUCID
HOUSE PUBLISHING

Published by Lucid House Publishing, LLC, Atlanta, Georgia, United States of America
www.LucidHousePublishing.com

Copyright 2021 © Douglas Thompson and Echo Montgomery Garrett

First Edition. All rights reserved. Printed in the United States.
This title is also available as an e-book via Lucid House Publishing, LLC

Cover and interior design: Amit Dey
Authors' photos: Andrea Nordhoff and Kevin Garrett

A Note to the Reader: Every effort has been made to ensure that the information contained in this book is complete and accurate. The content is based on the personal experiences of the author during his five decades in sales. It is published for general reference and education with the intent of inspiring hope, increasing resilience, and offering encouragement. The book is sold with the understanding that neither the authors nor the publisher are engaged in rendering any professional services including legal, psychological, career, or medical advice to the individual reader. The authors and publisher specifically disclaim any liability, loss, damage, injury or risk, directly or indirectly, for advice, suggestions, and information presented within. Neither the authors nor the publisher assume responsibility for errors, inaccuracies, omissions, or inconsistencies. Some of the names and identifying details of people mentioned in this book have been changed.

Library of Congress Cataloging-in-Publication Data
Thompson, Douglas, 1950-
Garrett, Echo Montgomery, 1960-
Knock! Knock!/ lessons learned and stories shared/a ride-along with sales superstar Douglas Thompson /Douglas Thompson/Echo Montgomery Garrett –1st U.S. ed.

ISBN: 978-1-950495-07-8
LCCN: 2020918889

1. Sales Success 2. Career in Sales 3. Training 4. Positive Mental Attitude
5. Relationship Building 6. Customer Loyalty 7. Referrals 8. Business networks
9. Integrity 9. Entrepreneurship 10. Time Management

BUS058000
BUS066000
BUS012000

Dedication

To my wife, Shirley.

We had no idea where this new career in sales was going to take the two of us, but your early confidence and faith in me and your continued emotional and moral support the entire way has been the key to building a successful career in sales. You truly have always been the wind beneath my wings.

Three simple rules in life.

1. If you do not go after what you want, you'll never have it.
2. If you do not ask, the answer will always be no.
3. If you do not step forward, you will always be in the same place.

— Author Unknown

ROAD MAP

Introduction: Sales for Life. ix

Chapter 1: The Accidental Salesman 1

Chapter 2: Failure is not an Option 13

Chapter 3: Time's a Wastin' 21

Chapter 4: You Gotta Keep Score 25

Chapter 5: A Sales Job vs. a Sales Career 35

Chapter 6: The Golden Rules of Prospecting. 43

Chapter 7: Don't Be A Secret Agent 49

Chapter 8: The Key Ingredient of Super-charged Sales:
            Positive Mental Attitude 57

Chapter 9: Winners Never Stop Learning 67

Chapter 10: Teaching Moments 75

Chapter 11: Two Ears, One Mouth 81

Chapter 12: When Life Throws You a Curve, Lean Into It 91

Chapter 13: Seal the Deal 101

Chapter 14: Brand You. 109

Chapter 15: The Big Payoff of Investing in Relationships 119

Epilogue 127

Acknowledgements. 131

About the Authors 133

Index. 135

Introduction

Sales for Life

*"Success is one thing you can't pay for.
You buy it on the installment plan and
make payments EVERY day."*

–Zig Ziglar

For the past five decades I've made my living in sales, and an excellent one at that. I was able to do it in one of the toughest sales arenas out there: selling accident, health, and life insurance door-to-door. Most of these products involve insuring life events that nobody wants to think about—that is until I walk in the door. From day one, I decided I was going to make the sales process a fun experience for both myself and the consumer. And now for you, the reader.

In all my time in sales, I cannot recall meeting a single soul who told me of a childhood dream to be a salesperson. In fact, a lot of folks may even have a negative attitude toward the sales profession. I was determined to do my best to replace that preconceived notion with a positive one.

But even if you have an aversion to the very word *sales*, at some point in your life I guarantee you will find yourself needing to sell something. It may be your talents and expertise to a potential employer or client. You may wind up in a job where some aspect of it involves sales. Your role as a leader may involve selling your ideas to your team. Or after reading this book, you may understand the tremendous opportunities that a career in sales can yield—if you just approach it with the right mindset and with integrity.

Like most people, I had never even considered sales when I thought about my future. My purpose in sharing what I've learned in the course of my sales career is three-fold: First, to help reframe sales as a profession; second, to provide time-tested basic principles that have worked for five decades and continue to work today no matter what you are selling; and third, to explore how being better at sales can make your life better and make sure you have a great time doing it.

I invite you to join me on what salespeople call "a ride along", which is where a senior salesperson shows a newbie the ropes. This book delivers a winning sales philosophy illustrated by real life stories and *Knock-Knock* moments from the career I feel so blessed to have.

Every sales encounter is initiated by a salesperson starting a conversation, regardless of whether it is face-to-face, on the phone, or virtual. Yet most people recoil from the thought of making that first move. Invariably, I hear some variation of: "Doug, I could never do that."

My reply: "Tell me your best Knock-Knock joke."

As soon as they do, a big smile comes across their face as they realize that they just initiated a conversation with an icebreaker most of us learned early in our childhood.

Some still protest: "But I could never do this door-to-door like you do."

My response: "You have likely already done it, but you have just forgotten. Did you ever go trick-or-treating? Almost every child was trained to be a door-to-door salesperson that one night in October. You walked up to a home, knocked on the door and started a conversation, and you were rewarded for it. Somewhere along the way, you grew an aversion to those skills and tactics you learned as a kid."

Ultimately, *Knock! Knock!* is about an attitude adjustment: Decide that you want to be the person with a positive mental attitude and heaps of gratitude. Sprinkled throughout I've included some of the comical situations I've found myself in and how I usually found a way to turn them around. Or at the very least, I'll share what those experiences taught me.

Throughout this book, I hope to help you overcome any aversions to sales and bring a smile to your face every time you read or hear one of my Knock-Knock experiences and stories. Each chapter concludes with Knock-Knock Moments—lessons and revelations that have fueled my career and that will help yours.

Every day presents a new opportunity to learn to be the best you can be in whatever selling career you find yourself in.

Chapter One

The Accidental Salesman

"If you can dream it, you can do it."

– Walt Disney

I was born on Christmas Eve in a town on the Texas-Oklahoma border. A happy-go-lucky kid, I have always looked at life as a gift.

Growing up, I never gave much thought to what I wanted to be. I certainly never considered a career in sales. Virtually no one plans to go into sales. They either follow family ties, stumble into it, or are recruited into it.

When I was nine years old, we left family and friends behind when Dad was transferred to Baker, Montana—a small town in Eastern Montana just twelve miles from North Dakota—to work on Shell Oil's pipeline. His job was to oversee the flow of all of the crude oil from northern Montana to southern Wyoming that went into that pipeline and then was pumped south to the refineries.

Mother quickly discovered that the local grocery in Montana didn't stock some of the items she considered staples for her Southern dishes. But she convinced the owner to order canned black-eyed peas, grits, and other items that appealed to the hundreds of Southerners who had made Baker a boomtown.

We hunted and fished all the time. Our freezer was packed with wild game—deer, antelope, and elk—so we always had meat on the table. And Mother quickly learned how to cook it all to perfection.

Dad always said, "Son, find as good of a cook as you were raised by."

With the five weeks of summer vacation came visits to Granny and Grandad's in central Oklahoma—Mother's father was a mechanic and welder in the oil industry—and on Dad's side Grandma and Grandad, who lived on Lake Texoma and were farmers.

Family was really important. My parents wanted my sister (younger by eleven months) and me to stay in touch with our Southern roots, so every summer we would drive all the way down South and spend five weeks of Dad's vacation with relatives. I looked forward to those long summer days, visiting with lots of aunts, uncles, and cousins—some in Oklahoma and some in Texas.

What I didn't look forward to each summer was the 25-hour drive to Oklahoma in Dad's old Pontiac with no air-conditioning. My mother would pack ground-venison-spread sandwiches in a cooler, and off we'd go. We never stopped at motels and seldom stopped at a restaurant. Dad didn't want to spend the time or the money.

It was a real splurge when we stopped for gas, and Dad instructed, "Go buy yourself a soda. Giddyup." My sister and I chugged down our icy-cold RC Colas by the pump, because Dad didn't want to pay the extra 5¢ for the bottle deposit.

Successfully identifying what I *didn't* want to do for a career

In Baker, your career choice was either to work on a ranch or in the oil field. We lived on the edge of town, with the wild Montana prairie as my backyard to play in.

The summer before I started high school, I hired out to a rancher as a ranch hand. My job was supposed to be helping him bale hay for his cattle. I figured it would be a good way to earn money for a car and get in shape for football.

Working on a ranch may sound romantic, but the nonstop work and 12-hour days gets old real fast.

On the first day he taught me how to milk the cow and informed me that this chore was now mine. So every morning, all summer long, I was up before daybreak milking that cow. We ate a good breakfast and then spent the long days either on a horse tending stock or baling hay. It was hot, dusty work. If you were out in the field, you didn't eat again until the evening meal. That didn't sit too well with a growing boy who was used to his mama cooking three great squares a day.

Now keep in mind, I was not an experienced ranch hand. I was a city slicker—if you can be such a thing in a town of 3,500 people way out in Eastern Montana.

On top of that, the job shifted from what I originally signed up for. A monsoon hit right as he was cutting the hay that his cattle would feed on all winter. The fields were flooded. That meant we had to herd the cattle down from the mountain meadows and get them back down to feed on the cut hay, or it would rot in the fields. You usually only move cattle twice a year, but this was no ordinary year.

So right off the bat, I was introduced to the horse that I would be riding all summer: a beautiful young paint named Susie. Now, I had never ridden a horse for more than ten minutes outside of a carnival up until this point. Susie, as well as the other horses on this ranch, were well-trained cutting horses that knew how to move cattle.

How hard could it be? "Just climb on and let the horse do the work," said the rancher. What he failed to tell me that first day on the range was that this little paint had been bitten by a rattlesnake when she was a colt and was scared to death of snakes—and any noise that remotely sounded like one.

I was riding along, pushing this herd of cows across the pasture, when a bird came flying out of a bush to my left. My horse hopped sideways three feet to the right, trying to get away from the noise. But I didn't go with her, and so down I went. I quickly climbed back on, embarrassed that I fell off a horse.

As we continued to move these little doggies across the pasture, at the next rustle of some brush she jumped sideways again, but this time to the left. Once again, I hit the dirt.

I looked up from the ground at the rancher. He said, "Oh, I forgot to tell you she's scared of rattlesnakes. You might want to hang on tighter."

I eventually realized you cannot ride twelve hours a day, six days a week, holding on for dear life. I hit the ground quite often in a day. I never once got bucked off this horse, but I found myself on the ground more times than you can shake a stick at.

Later in the summer when we were herding the cattle back up to the mountain meadows, we came across a stream swollen from the snow runoff and heavy thunderstorms we'd been having. My horse put her head down as we came to the stream. I waited because I thought she was drinking water. About the time I realized she wasn't she leapt from a still position and tried to make it all the way across that stream. This time I took a dunk in the cold mountain water.

The rancher looked back and said, "Oh, I forgot to tell you. She hates water almost as much as snakes. She almost drowned as a foal."

I hadn't signed on to be a cowboy, and here I was stuck with a horse that didn't want to be ridden and cattle that didn't want to be managed.

I had a choice. I could have called my dad and asked him to come get me, or I could suck it up and do what I had to do to make it to the end of summer. What I learned from that experience was that whatever you think a job entails and the actuality of what it requires is usually not the same. You have to adjust and adjust quickly.

Once I accepted that notion, I started enjoying what I was doing. It was an adventure every single day. The one thing I could count on was that my cutting horse would give me a wild ride. If you learn to be flexible, you can have fun no matter what.

In two-and-a-half months on the ranch, we never went to town. At the end of that summer, the rancher wrote me one big check. I took that check and bought my own car. I was the only kid in my freshman class who had a car that wasn't bought by Mom and Dad.

Growing up in Montana, I often went to work with Dad when he was on call for the oil field. I didn't mind it too much, except in the winter. The alarm system would sound in the middle of the night at the height of a blizzard, signaling that snow had blown up into the motors running the pipeline. The technician monitoring the pipeline would then call and alert Dad.

Once when I was 15 years old, Dad shook me awake at 2:30 in the morning during a white-out blizzard. "Wake up, Doug," he said. "Get dressed. We gotta go."

I knew the drill. My job was to keep the pickup truck's motor running and the headlights trained on Dad to help him see what he was doing. The wind would be blowing so hard that the snow and frigid temperatures could kill the motor on the pickup if you weren't careful.

Well, I sat there in the truck with the heater on full blast, watching my dad doing his job in 30 degrees below 0 temperatures with the wind and snow whipping.

As I sat in that pickup truck that night I thought, *I don't know what I'm going to do the rest of my life, but it ain't going to be this.*

My athletic dreams are crushed

I was a jock and lettered in football, basketball, and track all four years of high school. Our town's football program had experienced a huge turn-around, and during my high school years we only lost one game. My senior year, I was selected as All-Conference at the center position for Montana's High School football. As a result, I was offered a full-ride football scholarship to Minot State in North Dakota, about 300 miles from home.

I planned on majoring in math and industrial engineering which caught my attention in high school, where I'd spent four years taking architectural drafting.

The only problem? I played basketball, too, and in a regional tournament on our way to the state championship my senior year, I blew my knee out. I tried to quickly rehab the knee but only got to play one game in the state tournament, which likely damaged it further.

I did my best to rehab it myself that summer before showing up for spring football training on Minot's campus. But it blew again after just two days on the football team. "You'll need to get that fixed before the season starts," my coach said.

My heart sank a few days later when I found out how bad the injury was and that it would require major surgery, which in those days pretty much ended your athletic career. My coach allowed me to finish out my freshman year on scholarship.

Is this the best way to do this?

I transferred to Montana State University in Bozeman, where I continued to draw up schematics of manufacturing plants as an industrial engineering major. I was fascinated with the idea of helping existing businesses do what they did, better, faster, more safely, and more economically.

Our professors gave us case studies and then posed the question: "What would you recommend the business change?"

Another important principle they taught was the reality that sometimes the world's not ready for change. One of my professors told this story as an example:

Crisco was a popular kitchen staple, especially among Southern cooks. When you opened up the can, about a teaspoon-size dab of the shortening stuck to the lid. An industrial engineer with Crisco came up with the bright idea that the company could save some money by eliminating that small waste on the lid. Sales started falling immediately and complaints started rolling in. *You changed the cooking oil. It tastes different. My fried chicken isn't as crispy.*

The truth was, not a single thing had changed about the product except that small dab of shortening no longer clung to the lid. Finally, Crisco's executives decided to change the label, adding the words: *Back to the original formula!* And most importantly, they made flat-dab sure that every can of Crisco had that little dab of shortening stuck to the lid. Sales recovered quickly, and Crisco continued to dominate its category with the housewives of America.

I loved learning and thinking about all these case studies. The idea of going into manufacturers in order to improve their automation fit my personality. I've always tried to figure out: *Is this the best way to do this?*

Over Christmas break during my second year in college, I came home and worked in the oil field. One of the young men just five years older than me, working on a workover rig, was missing two fingers. They used chains to wrap around the pipe to tighten each piece on these rigs. His hand had gotten caught once while throwing these chains and with one quick jerk he was scarred for life.

There weren't a lot of safety regulations in that industry back then, plus the harsh Montana weather beat you up every day. That oil field job on my college break made a lasting impression on me and underscored my desire for another way to make a living.

I finished my sophomore year, and then my education hit another roadblock. Every break I was working and saving every dime for college, but without that football scholarship it simply wasn't enough.

Sometimes the best education comes in the form of on-the-job training

My grandparents and aunt and uncle owned property at Lake Havasu, Arizona. I quit college, just temporarily, to earn some better money laying water and sewer lines out in the middle of the desert as they worked to build this new town. This was my first exposure to union work, and it made me *not* a fan of unions. Every three to six months, workers had to go back to the union hall and wait for their next assignment even though there was still work to be done with this employer. But I made such an impression on the owner and management of this company by the end of my first six-month stint that the owner said, "If we make you a foreman we can keep you on, son."

At only 21 years old, my new role meant I would be managing people old enough to be my father, but I took the challenge on. The union rules made it tough on companies, because you had to retrain your workforce every three months. You couldn't keep those people you'd developed, and it was a vicious cycle.

That led to an offer from John McCulloch, who had purchased the London Bridge in England and moved it to Arizona and was rebuilding it piece by piece. So I worked for a year-and-a-half putting the London Bridge back together again.

Whenever I wasn't working on the bridge I pitched in to help out my grandparents, who operated a motel, and my aunt and uncle, who operated a gas station/liquor store/mini-mart/bait shop down by the lake.

Half of the motel was bachelor quarters for all the construction workers who were in town, where I lived rent-free. Each room had two beds and two closets with a huge common bathroom down the hall—kind of like a college dorm. Whenever I wasn't working on the London Bridge, I earned my keep by working as a housekeeper at the motel, then on weekends selling liquor, and handing out bait at the mini-mart.

When my granddad, who ran the hotel, died of cancer, we took him back to be buried in Oklahoma. While I was there, my mother's brother offered me a job in Texas related to my desire to be an engineer. "Lufkin Industries will put you to work and pay for your schooling," he said.

That sounded like a good deal to me. The company was known worldwide for building those horse-head pumping units you would see in the oil fields. But what I worked on at Lufkin were huge marine transmissions or gear reducers for oil tankers. Each master gear was 20 to 25 feet tall. If one of these oil tankers broke down in the middle of the ocean, we sent out a company engineer to help repair it. This was what I was being trained to do.

I was working from 3:30 pm to midnight building these gear reducers and continuing my studies for my engineering degree during the day. One afternoon before my shift, I stopped in this grocery store across from the factory for snacks and food. A petite, platinum blonde cashier caught my eye.

When she handed me my change, I thought her fingers lingered before she turned away to help the next customer. I became a regular after that and made sure I got in her line each time.

Before long, I worked up my courage to ask Shirley out on a date. As I made my approach, I heard one of her coworkers whisper loudly, "That guy is in here looking at you again."

After our first date, we dated regularly. Before long I asked Shirley to marry me, and she said yes.

I called my parents in Montana to tell them I had met the woman of my dreams, a true Southern belle, and to invite them to our wedding. Dad's first question was: "Is she really a Southern gal?"

"Dad, she is as good of a cook as Mom, and she is from so far back in these East Texas swamps that she has water rings around her ankles."

They congratulated us and said they would fly down.

I was only 24, and all I owned in the world was a brand new, two-seater red sports car and a motorcycle. Now all of the sudden, I was committing to getting married and having a family to support. I took a second job working at Safeway. I was burning the candle at both ends. Working two jobs and trying to go to school was making some long twenty-hour days.

One night I was riding my motorcycle home after my midnight shift, and I came within a whisper of being a speck on the back of a truck that didn't have working brake lights and failed to signal a left-hand turn. Plus, I had already been run off the road dodging traffic a couple of times at that same time of night.

In that split second, I realized I couldn't keep working that kind of schedule.

Shortly after that wake-up call, I answered a blind ad in the newspaper. It advertised that the company was "looking for a sports-minded individual".

It didn't say much else, and Longview was about 100 miles from where Shirley and I both lived. *I'm competitive and will go head-to-head playing just about anything.* I was intrigued.

I owned one white dress shirt and one tie, but I didn't own a suit jacket. As was the style in the early 1970s, my hair was down to my shoulders and I had a mustache and a goatee.

The interview was held in a motel room at a Holiday Inn in this East Texas town. The local manager doing the interviewing explained that I would be selling their company's product by going door-to-door, calling on businesses, selling these products in every town in every county in East Texas.

He told me how they sold the product, but still hadn't told me what I would be selling. He told me how much I could make selling this product. When I tried to ask him what the product was, he said, "We'll get to that in just a minute."

About that time the assistant manager comes into the room to go to lunch. This guy looks like he couldn't chew gum and walk at the same time. "That's one of our trainers," my interviewer said.

"Why don't you let me do a ride-along in the field with him, so I can see how this whole program works?" I asked.

The interviewer said, "Go for it."

Once we got out there, I realized he was selling an individual workers comp type accident insurance plan to owners and managers of small businesses. The first business owner couldn't meet with us, the second threw us out, but the third time was a home run. He sold the policy, and the owner thanked him over and over again for coming by.

So, in those three cold-calls I got to see what the product they were selling actually was, and how it was supposed to work from his presentations. Now, from working on ranches, oil fields and construction jobs, I could see that an accident policy that paid you cash money if you got hurt and couldn't work actually made a lot of sense.

"Okay, I've seen enough," I said. "Let's go back to the Holiday Inn."

When I sat down with the manager, I said, "I'll give it a go. If this guy can do it, I can."

He said, "If you will get a haircut and a shave, we'll hire you."

My most important sales presentation ever

The thrill I felt dwindled a bit on the two-hour drive home as I rehearsed how to tell my fiancée that I was quitting two paying jobs and giving up on college to take a sales job that paid straight commissions and would require us to move 100 miles away to Longview.

Well, I gave her quite a sales presentation. I explained all of those details. I told her what I'd be doing and that I'd get to manage my own time and be my own boss. I explained what I could make and assured her that I felt I'd be on the high end of their projections.

Then I told her I had to get my insurance license and travel to Dallas for a week-long school. "Oh, and by the way, during that month to six weeks, I will not be bringing home any weekly income," I said. "Then upon completion of getting an insurance license and graduating from the insurance training program, we'll be living on straight commissions based on what I sell each week."

I concluded, "In other words, we will no longer have any guaranteed income from here on out."

Shirley asked a few good questions. "Tell me again how you get paid and when you get paid," she replied. Her questions were the same ones I had had.

Then, without a pause, she said, "I know you can do it, and you should go for it."

I had only known Shirley for less than a year, but she apparently knew me better than I knew myself, because I was scared to death.

As promised, my parents flew in for our wedding. Waiting at the airport for their arrival, Shirley was a little nervous about meeting my mom and dad. Mom came running up and gave her a good ol' hug. Dad walked up, bent down and pulled her pants leg up, and said, "Show me those water rings around your ankles, girl!"

In September 1974, a year to the day after our first date, we got married in the same church by the same preacher who married my mom and dad in Denison, Texas.

We launched into the next chapter of our life with no idea of what our future would bring.

Knock-Knock Moments

- Sometimes working a job and finding out that it isn't for you is the best way to discover your true calling. Pay attention to your personal satisfaction and ask yourself, "Does this feel like a good fit for me?"

- Each time you make a move, figure out what that experience taught you. You might be in the right job and have the wrong boss, or vice versa. Look at what went well and what didn't.

- Keep your options open. Don't get locked up by the expectations of others.

- Take the long view.

Chapter Two

Failure is not an Option

"Nothing in the world can take the place of persistence. Talent will not; nothing is more common than unsuccessful men with talent. Genius will not; unrewarded genius is almost a proverb. Education will not; the world is full of educated derelicts. Persistence and determination alone are omnipotent. The slogan Press On! has solved and always will solve the problems of the human race."

– Calvin Coolidge

Everybody around you is going to be a naysayer when you go into sales—especially if your income is straight commission. Prepare to have your career choice questioned a lot by friends, relatives, and even strangers. On top of that, getting your sales career off the ground is going to take a ton of good old-fashioned hard work. To be good at sales, you have to study your product, learn the basic sales skills, and then keep building from there.

I had always been a C+ student. Not because I wasn't smart but because I didn't apply myself. I only did the homework I had to do. I seldom did any extra work or made an additional effort to study in order to make better grades. I skated through school.

Unfortunately, the same attitude, approach, and study habits almost stopped my career in insurance sales before it even got started. I had to obtain my insurance license before I was eligible to attend the company's week-long school in Dallas. This was a self-study process so I ordered the books and paid the fee, which was more money going out than we could afford.

Failure is not fatal

I scanned through these books like you might do when preparing for a driver's license test. I took the test, which required a 70 as a passing grade. I got a 68. I paid the testing fee again, and this time I actually read and studied the contents of these books. This go-round I scored only a 66 on the test.

What in the world? I was perplexed because I'd actually studied this time, at least I thought I did, but I scored worse. Now I was in deep trouble. In Texas, you are only allowed to take the test three times. If you fail all three attempts, you then have to wait six months to take it again.

I had already quit college and both my jobs. My fiancée was counting on me to make this work.

I studied and studied that book with the deadline of the upcoming company school in Dallas looming. If I did not pass that Texas insurance exam that week, I would be terminated from this opportunity. I paid the testing fee one more time, burned the midnight oil, and took the test again.

This time I passed with flying colors. At least that is what I told myself even though I only got a 78. But seriously, I realized that I had terrible study habits. *If I cannot do better than this, I've made a very poor decision choosing insurance sales as a career.*

In the past, I could not handle memorizing anything well. I was the last student in the sixth grade to stand at the front of the class and recite Lincoln's *Gettysburg Address*. I just could not memorize it. Plus, I was scared to death to be in front of my classmates and possibly embarrass myself.

When I got to the Dallas training school, I found out that I had to memorize an entire presentation, the rebuttals, and the closes. Then I had to present them perfectly, word-for-word, in front of every other student, or I would not pass. Upon hearing that news, I almost walked out that first night.

In fact, I almost walked out every evening. I did terribly those first few days. I was one of the worst in the class. I just could not get this stuff memorized. At least three times, I sat in my car in the parking lot and said, "Doug, you need to go home and go back to work."

But I kept reminding myself that I had told my wife-to-be that I could do this, and I had quit both jobs as well as quitting school. All my eggs were in this insurance sales basket, and I could not afford to fail.

> **"Many people fail not so much because of their mistakes,
> they fail because they are afraid to try."**
>
> **— George Foreman**

Let your competitive spirit be a driver

Not only was I very competitive in sports, but I loved to compete in any other games I could get someone to play. It didn't matter if it was chess, checkers, or Monopoly. But school had never seemed hard to me. It was not a challenge and certainly did not seem competitive, so I always had trouble keeping focused on it.

This school was different. Each day more and more of my classmates dropped out of the program. But when I made the connection that the more I learned what they were teaching in insurance school today, the more money I could make tomorrow, my competitive spirit kicked in and I buckled down.

After I graduated from insurance school in Dallas, something changed in me.

I had a revelation. Everything about the sales profession was competitive. It was a competition to walk in cold and fight to get the client's attention. It was a competition to get them to allow me to give them a presentation on the spot. It was competitive to convince them of the need for my product, and then it was like shooting the winning shot at the buzzer to close that sale before they could convince themselves that they did not need it.

The first company I was with recruited quite a few potential sales-people at a time, expecting that most of them would wash out during that intense week in insurance sales school that I had miraculously survived.

The first day of on-the-job training at our Monday morning break-fast meeting in a small town in East Texas, there were too many sales neophytes that first morning for the two managers to take on sales calls. One of the three of us was going to have to sit tight. The manager seemed relieved when I volunteered to wait for my turn to be field-trained until after lunch.

But after about an hour, I had had way too much coffee. Plus, I was growing more and more antsy. I decided that since I had my assignment of what area I was to cover, and I'd done a few ride-alongs with a manager the day I interviewed, I should just go ahead and hit the street.

Besides, I reasoned, I'd spent an entire week practicing every aspect of my presentation over and over again. You can practice all you want, but until you get in the game you don't really know how good you are going to be.

I parked my car on a side street in my assigned portion of town, got out, took a deep breath and hurried into the first business I came to, as I did not want to allow myself any time to get nervous. This was a plumb-ing supply business owned by a nice couple. The wife was sitting at the front counter. Well, not only did I sell her, but she bought a policy for her husband as well. I left that business walking on air and in a daze. I had done it! I had actually followed each step I had learned, and it worked.

Well not only did I sell those folks, but I sold a policy on the next sales call and the next one. By this time, I was in a zone. I couldn't have told you where I was or what time of the day it was. I no longer felt nervous. In fact, I felt like kicking the next door in.

Then BAM, as I was walking down the sidewalk, I heard a voice say, "Where have you been, Doug?" A car had pulled up and I saw my manager, looking very perturbed. "You were supposed to wait for me at the restaurant, and I've been looking all over this town for you. Just what do you think you are doing?"

"Well, sir, I knew what my area was, so I thought I'd give it try and just got busy making some sales," I said. "Sorry."

"You mean you made a sale?" he asked, eyes wide.

"Actually, I've sold three so far."

I looked at Jenny, the new agent I had just completed school with, who was sitting beside him and being trained by this manager all morning and asked, "How many have you guys sold so far?"

"Zero," she replied, and turned and looked at the manager.

Well, he was already sweating from being out all morning in this Texas summer heat, and he flushed redder than a mortgage-buster tomato. He stumbled with his words and muttered that maybe I should just keep on doing what I was doing. "I will see you at 5:30 sharp back at the restaurant," he said, and drove off.

Long story short, I worked by myself the entire first week without ever riding with either of the managers and made twice as many sales as all of the other new agents in our crew put together.

The second week, I rode with the manager one day. We made some sales, so he was now a happy camper and was able to report that he had field-trained me.

Keeping score

I had struggled to pass the insurance test. Then I struggled even worse at insurance school trying to learn this material and was discouraged by seeing so many other classmates in the program, who I admired, give up.

But I decided early on that the only way to thrive in this career was to keep a positive mental attitude. At that first breakfast meeting, the manager spent that hour priming us for success by pumping positive sayings into our minds and encouraging us.

Each day ended the same way. He spent another hour letting us share our best moments of the day and discussing what we could do better by learning from each other's mistakes.

Everyone was now keeping score. You met with your team and field manager three times a day: every morning to get your new street assignments; at lunch to review your results; and again at 5:30 for an hour of additional training and to go over the day's results. You competed against the fellow agents on your team, but you also competed with all the other agents with this company in Texas. The managers and the home office both kept score of your sales. They gave awards each week and each month to the top salesperson, and news flyers came out weekly showing who the top producers were. Now *this* kind of competition motivated me.

Most importantly, my family now kept score. Every night when I got home my new wife wanted to know how my day went, and I did not want to disappoint the person who had so much faith in me to begin with. So if I had a bad day selling I would make extra cold calls at the end of each day on the way home, trying to score a sale to make sure I walked into that front door with a positive attitude and a kick in my step knowing I had brought home a gain that day. Her big smile and hug the minute I came in the house was more than enough to keep me going.

You have to understand, I made more money in those first two days than I was making in a week working two jobs. I set a company record for the state of Texas for my first week and for my first month's production by a new agent. I made more my first month than anyone else in the company ever had done in a given month.

Based on my rocky start, I was probably the last guy anyone would have bet on.

Knock-Knock Moments

- Don't let the naysayers get you down. Don't listen to them.
- You can't win the game if you don't stay in it.
- Sometimes the biggest victory comes from simply not giving up.
- Find a daily scorecard that motivates you.

Chapter Three

Time's a Wastin'

"You've got to know what you want. This is central to acting on your intentions. When you know what you want, you realize that all there is left then is time management. You'll manage your time to achieve your goals, because you clearly know what you're trying to achieve in your life."

– Patch Adams

At the end of the sixth week into my new sales job, I got a jolt of reality when my commission check came. With this company and earning straight commissions, you got paid the following week for the new policies you'd written and turned in the previous week.

Keep in mind, we'd been living paycheck-to-paycheck. Plus, I had quit those two jobs almost two months earlier, so money was tight. We were making our bills, but just barely. Suddenly, we had more money than we had ever thought we would make. Because of what I had learned and made work, and then saw what it produced, I got the feeling that I'd tapped into a well that never runs dry. But I forgot that you've got to keep priming the pump.

After breaking all kinds of company records with my hot start and bringing home four to five times a week what I had previously made working *two* jobs, I committed the cardinal sin of sales.

Keep showing up and putting in the work

My new bride and I fell into a trap common to the newly self-employed, now responsible for their own schedule and productivity for the first time. And that's how you should think of yourself if you are in sales. Anybody who is an independent contractor in any line of business must realize that your success all comes down to your sales and how much time you invest in that aspect of your business. Because, regardless of what you create, manufacture or service, you are in sales as well.

How you manage your time as a salesperson is up to you. You are not punching a time clock. If I didn't go to work one day because I had a lot of items on my honey-do list, or if I failed to show up at the Monday morning meeting, that was all on me. It felt good being my own boss, but I had yet to recognize all the responsibility that comes with that honor.

By the end of my first month as a commissioned salesman, we got too busy spending money and running errands.

Then on that fifth week, that next check came.

Instead of a WOW moment, it was a WOE moment! We barely had enough money to cover groceries for the week.

What the heck happened? I had filled up my schedule with so many other things that I barely took the time to work. I forgot that my main job was to focus on making the sales that generated that nice income. I lost track of my numbers.

Well, you better believe that my drive to make sales returned in a hurry. I put the brakes on saying "yes" to a long list of honey-dos. Those errands that had seemed so urgent could wait.

Your hunger to make it financially will determine the number of days and the amount of time you put in. I learned real fast that there is a direct correlation between your paycheck and how you prioritize your schedule.

I also discovered that you cannot afford to take shortcuts. When you've gotten behind on your sales goal, your inclination is to try and hurry up the process. I found myself jumping from step 1 to step 4 and expecting to get positive results. By skipping steps, I started getting a lot more rejections and hearing "no" over and over again way too often.

Funny how that works. Would-be customers sense when you are pushing too hard. Once they get a whiff of desperation, you are toast.

I had to go back to the tried-and-true formula that I had been using those first four weeks for sales success. And that meant taking control of my time management instead of letting my wasted time control my sales activity. No more rushing the sales process.

Poor time management is your enemy

Lack of good time management has always been a huge evil presence in the sales industry. If you put off what you should be doing first, nine out of ten times it will come back to haunt you.

The agents who made a habit of skipping the Monday motivational meetings and regularly took time off in the early part of the week would lose track and control of their time and goals, which invariably landed them at the bottom of the pile when it came to performance.

I prepared myself to come out of the gate hot first thing after the Monday morning meeting. I focused solely on making calls and obtaining sales results. I found that I was much more likely to meet my sales goals for the week if I busted it early in the week. Then, if I'd exceeded that goal by Thursday, I would sometimes elect to take Friday off as a reward.

Once we had our children, I rarely missed any sort of activity, whether it was an athletic event or school talent show. Many times, I was the only dad there in the middle of the day. However, I carefully planned my time so that if I was in the school auditorium from 10 am until noon, I made up for those hours with additional sales calls at the end of the day. Or, later in my management career, went back to work in my office after the children's bedtime. There is no substitute for putting the time in.

By learning to balance my schedule and use my time wisely, I got the best of both worlds: success in sales and quality time with my family. That's the best payoff ever.

Knock-Knock Moments

- Time is your most valuable asset. Don't waste it. Ever.
- Prioritize your schedule before Monday rolls around.
- Develop discipline in your schedule.

Chapter 4

You Gotta Keep Score

*"If it doesn't matter who wins or loses,
then why do they keep score?"*

– Vince Lombardi

At my first sales job, I learned one of the biggest secrets to sales success: Track your numbers. Religiously. No excuses, period. As a jock, the idea of keeping score appealed to me. Once I made it a habit in sales, I found it be a game-changer.

The ironic thing is that today I rarely find sales organizations that teach this one simple tactic. In fact, when recruiting salespeople, I frequently encounter those who refuse to give numbers, citing their "independence" as the reason.

That's a big fat red flag. If you fail to keep a scorecard, it's way too easy to fool yourself into thinking you are doing a decent job when you may be way off the mark and don't even know why.

Track the right numbers

In my first job, the reporting process called for all salespeople to track the following on a daily basis:

- How many calls you made
- The number of presentations you made

- How many closes you did
- And how many sales you made as a result

Those four numbers provided you and your manager a daily snapshot of your progress. In every local agency office, there was a blackboard with agents' names and their numbers. On Monday morning, everybody in the office could see how you did the previous week.

You could also tell if somebody was trying to make numbers up, because they wouldn't have the results to support their claims.

This system kept you honest and accountable. It also revealed where you needed to improve. For example, you could look at what the average agent was doing in the office and see how you stacked up. Let's say the average in the office was that an agent made 100 calls, made 60 presentations, did 30 closes, and netted 15 sales.

But let's say you matched all those numbers, except you had a buckshot for sales. Either you were the worst closer in the history of the company, or you fudged your numbers. If you don't properly track your numbers, the most important person you are cheating is yourself. I am always surprised when people don't make that connection.

Hold yourself accountable

After that really terrible week when I got such a small commission check and we could barely eat, I diligently tracked my numbers. Once I understood how important those numbers could be, after each appointment I'd have either what I called a steering wheel review with myself or with my senior manager if that person was doing a ride-along with me.

Because I had such a poor memory, I kept that scorecard in my shirt pocket. While it was still fresh in my mind, I jotted down a review on what had gone well and what could have gone better. After each action I took, I ticked it off on the scorecard.

I learned the hard way that if you wait until the end of the day, you forget important details. By regularly reviewing those notes, I could discern where I needed to improve.

Here is the information I designed on 3x5 cards to keep score, which matched the blackboard numbers required at each Monday morning meeting:

	Mon	Tue	Wed	Thurs	Fri	Sat
Phone calls made						
Door Knocks made						
Presentations made						
Closes given						
Sales Made						
Referrals Obtained						
Total Premium written						
Total Commissions earned						

By keeping track of these numbers, agents could answer the seven questions below and know at a glance where they stood on goals and where they needed improvement:

- What are your numbers?
- What are your ratios?
- What is the average commission of each of your sales?
- How many sales do you need to hit your weekly goals?
- What is your best day to sell?
- What is your best time to sell? Morning or afternoon?
- Do you ask for referrals on every call?

Depending on your business and your role in sales, you may need to track different categories. However, this example from the insurance industry gives you a good place to start. There are several different software tracking systems, some specific to an industry, that allow you to track your numbers. Salesforce.com is one of the best I've found.

Numbers never lie

When you get all the steps down pat for making a successful sale, watch out. You can easily fall into a rut, or you can go the other direction and start going off-script without realizing you are doing it.

Once I got rolling again and was back to breaking records, I got a little too full of myself. How did I know? My sales were off based on the number of closes I was doing. When I got gut-level honest with myself, I was overtalking during the close and trying to infuse too much humor into the presentation.

I wasn't getting paid to make people laugh. I was getting paid to sell them an insurance policy. Now, while I believed we both needed to make sure this was a fun experience, my attempts at humor were losing people instead of sealing the deal.

GOALS! What are your short- and long-term goals?

Why Set Goals? Top-level athletes, successful businesspeople, and achievers in all fields all have one thing in common: They **set goals**. Setting **goals** gives you long-term vision and short-term motivation.

Goals help you focus on what knowledge you need to acquire. They help you organize your time and your resources, so that you can make the most of your efforts.

Can you imagine boarding a flight, and the captain steps out of the cockpit and asks: "Well, folks, where do y'all want to go today?" As Yogi Berra once said: "If you don't know where you are going, you'll end up someplace else".

While we are going to be talking about the importance of setting goals in sales, keep in mind that individuals come up with all kinds of goals. What motivates one person might not appeal to you at all or would never occur to you. In the course of my career probably the oddest goal that I have ever come across involved a salesperson named Rose, who was staffing a kiosk in a retail store in Tennessee for my company.

I got a complaint from the manager of the store that we might have a lady of the night working in our kiosk. I chalked this up as a prank call, but a couple days later the store manager called me with the same complaint and went into great detail about why he felt this way.

This issue had now escalated and needed to be investigated ASAP. I happened to already be in this part of Tennessee working, so I stopped by Rose's kiosk to see what in the daylights the manager was talking about.

Keep in mind that all the insurance agents we have hired to work in these kiosks have a dress code requirement. We provided them a set of khaki slacks and a blue polo shirt with our company logo on it to wear while they are working.

When I walked into this store, I could not believe what I was seeing. Rose followed fellow Tennessean Dolly Parton's sense of style. A tall lady with long, platinum white hair, Rose was standing in front of this kiosk in knee-high white boots, a mini skirt, and a white blouse that highlighted her assets. I walked up to Rose, introduced myself and asked her how business was, and why she was not wearing the mandatory clothing we had sent her.

She said, "Douglas, my husband passed away four years ago, and I just turned 68 years old. I have decided I need a man in my life again. So my GOAL is to find a new boyfriend by Christmas, and the kiosk in front of this store is a great place to meet men."

For once, I was left speechless.

"A goal is a dream with a deadline."

– Napoleon Hill

How successful do you want to be?

People who write down their goals have an **80% higher** rate of achieving those goals compared to people who do not write down goals. Okay, okay. I know you've likely heard that startling statistic. But are you doing it? If not, why not?

Many of the most successful salespeople I know keep a photograph of something that motivates them where they see that image several times a day. It might be a photo of your family. Maybe it's a dream vacation home or a vintage sportscar. Whatever it is, keep a reminder of that goal front and center. Once you meet that goal, find something else that motivates you just as much.

> **"Think about your goals at every opportunity throughout the day."**
>
> **– Brian Tracy**

You need to set SMART goals, which are goals that are specific, measurable, achievable, relevant, and timebound. These specific criteria are easily remembered by using the acronym S-M-A-R-T. This concept has been taught, written about, and promoted by many great sales leaders and authors over the years.

How do you go about setting these types of goals? Provided below are three types of goals a salesperson should set:

- **Needs Goal**: your absolute minimum income and production requirements
- **Lifestyle Goal**: a target goal you need to live comfortably
- and a **Mount Everest Goal**: your stretch goal or dream income goal.

The process is the same for setting each type of goal. You just need to adjust the income requirements and the production necessary to achieve each one.

Instructions: Fill out the first three columns (income goals) for the three listed goals. If you have a sales manager, ask that person to help you fill in the remaining columns based on the amounts you want to make. Once you have established what your weekly income needs or goals are, then divide those by the average commissions you make per sale (in our industry, the measuring stick is based on a completed application).

Then you look at your daily scorecard to see how many appointments per week you need to reach X amount of sales. Then, once again using your daily scorecard, figure out how many sales calls you must make in a week to generate the number of presentations you need. Next, look at the number of closes you need to give in order to make, and finally, all of these numbers will lead you to the number of sales you will generate with this type of activity.

As your experience and sales skills improve so will the ratios on your scorecard, which means these goals will be easier to meet going forward.

Once these three goals are completed, make copies. Post one in your office, on your mirror, the dash of your car—wherever you will see your goals daily. Give one to your spouse or significant other. BE ACCOUNT-ABLE TO YOUR GOALS.

If you follow them, you will attain them!

Needs Goal (Minimum): How much do I NEED to live on? What is the smallest amount I can get by on? What is the amount that I NEED to pay my bills, i.e. housing, food, utilities, car?

Monthly Income	Annual Income (Monthly x 12)	Weekly Income (Annual ÷ 50)	Applications Per Week	Closes Given Per Week	Presentations made Per Week	Phone Calls/ Door Knocks Per Week

Lifestyle Goal (Target): How much do I need to be COMFORT-ABLE? How much money do I need per month to cover all of my needs and some of my wants (new shoes, entertainment, nice gifts for special occasions)?

Monthly Income	Annual Income (Monthly x 12)	Weekly Income (Annual ÷ 50)	Applications per Week	Closes Given Per Week	Presentations made Per Week	Phone Calls/ Door Knocks Per Week

Mount Everest Goal (Stretch): How much do I WANT to live on? What is my ideal monthly income to live my ideal lifestyle?

Monthly Income	Annual Income (Monthly x 12)	Weekly Income (Annual ÷ 50)	Applications Per Week	Closes Given Per Week	Presentations Made Per Week	Phone Calls/ Door Knocks Per Week

You may think keeping track of all those numbers sounds like too much work. Well let me tell you, it's worth every minute you spend on it. No matter what industry you are in, decide what numbers you should track on your scorecard. Then discipline yourself to write them down daily, even if nobody else around you is doing it. In fact, most sales organizations, sales managers, salespeople—veterans and newbies alike—or anyone who does sales as part of their job these days fail to put this simple tool to use. For me, I haven't found a better way yet to improve my performance as a sales professional and help those around me up their game than to keep score.

> **"What you get by achieving your goals is not as important as what you become by achieving your goals."**
>
> **– Zig Ziglar**

Knock-Knock Moments

- Figure out the best way to keep score and then use that tool religiously.
- Listen to the story the numbers are telling and adjust accordingly.
- Have a steering wheel review with yourself after every sales call.
- Review your goals daily.

Chapter Five

A Sales Job vs. A Sales Career

"I take a simple view of life: Keep your eyes open and get on with it."

– Sir Laurence Olivier

I rose up through the ranks pretty quickly with the first company that hired me as a salesman. Within the first three months, I was promoted to assistant manager for the area of East Texas that I was in.

Shortly thereafter, I was named district manager. I was responsible not only for my own sales, but also teaching and training other salespeople on all aspects of the sales process. Part of my job as a manager was prepping the town that was our next target.

Everybody was a prospect, just by virtue of the fact that they lived or worked on a street that was assigned to a particular salesperson. I'd sit down with a map and divvy up the town for my sales team, starting with what we called the "centers of influence." Our first stops were with the mayor, the chief of police, judges, and anybody who held a position of respect. Even if we couldn't get that person to buy, we'd ask their permission to speak to others in their employ or under their leadership. Then we'd namedrop throughout that town, giving us instant credibility.

Churn-and-burn never works long-term

Now, the only rub was that the company didn't want us "wasting" any time building relationships in a particular town. Our only job was to sell as many of these policies in each town that we could and move on to the next town ten miles down the road. With this churn-and-burn strategy, you never saw the same person twice.

As a 25-year-old my job of opening up each town had put me in a ton of knee-shaking positions, calling on some of the most powerful people in the state of Texas. You couldn't bypass that part of your job, because your team was counting on you. But I'd discovered that I could go one-on-one with any of these folks and do just fine.

After two-and-a-half years of this I saw the impact of that strategy. And it started gnawing on me that, although I was good at quickly gaining the trust of key influencers in a town, I didn't get an opportunity to make anything more of the relationship I built during these short encounters.

Then the company was bought out by a subsidiary of K-Mart, headquartered in Indiana, and a dozen of us top performers were brought to that state to compete for four top management positions.

The luck of draw gave me the assignment of the city hall in Indianapolis, which meant calling on the mayor. Most of the mayors in the small towns of East Texas that I'd called on were often still wearing their bib overalls from their full-time ranch jobs.

Unbeknownst to me, Mayor Richard Lugar presided over the city and the county, which had recently merged. His office was on the top floor of a new 28-story city/county building, the tallest building in Indianapolis.

I had never been on an elevator that went any higher than a few floors. That ride alone was worth the stop. I told his executive assistant what I wanted to speak to the mayor about. "Wait here," she said.

Less than a minute later, to my surprise she announced, "He'll see you now." She gestured toward a large walnut door.

Find a way to connect and build on that connection

When I entered the mayor's office, I saw that three of the walls were floor-to-ceiling glass. His desk was positioned in the middle of this enormous room. I felt like I could see the whole state of Indiana from up there.

I was sure he could see my heart pounding in my chest. I got three lines into my standard spiel before blurting out, "Sir, how can you get any work done up here?"

What I didn't know is that he had fought tooth and nail to get this building constructed and had been instrumental in its design and the lengthy approval process. He grinned, jumped up from his chair, and said, "Son, let me show you around." He pointed out different parts of the city and the state and told me the story of how he'd made it all happen.

I oohed and aahed and listened for the next thirty minutes or more. When we finally got back to his desk, he pointed at my brochure and said, "Go ahead, sir, with what you wanted to show me."

The mayor didn't buy a policy on himself, but when I asked his permission to speak to all city and county employees about our insurance offerings, he gave it on the spot. Securing the mayor's backing represented a huge win for our entire team and kept us busy for weeks to come. Not too much longer after my encounter with Mayor Richard Lugar, he became a senator for the state of Indiana where he served for 36 years and was presented the Presidential Medal of Freedom in 2013.

Something shifted for me that day. The more I thought about that career highpoint, the more I realized something important. The biggest sale of my career had come about by sheer accident. I had never been in a building that tall before, nor had I ever seen a view like that. I went off script, and he was flattered by my genuine interest in his office, his city, and his successful merger of the city and county. I'd made an important personal connection on that cold call.

We'd been drilled to keep moving. To not waste time and stay focused on the sale. Period. End of story.

From that point on, I had a problem drinking the company Kool-Aid and selling the hit-and-run strategy. But I ignored that gnawing in my gut, accepted the promotion, and moved my pregnant wife to Indianapolis where our daughter was born.

I recruited, hired, trained, and built up a successful sales team for Indianapolis. Just when I got everything rolling with that group, the company moved us to Muncie. I was there six months, recruiting and building a team, and then I was told that my next territory would be Fort Wayne. I uprooted my family once again. But it kept eating at me that not only was I not allowed to build relationships with clients, but now I couldn't even build and keep a strong relationship with my sales team.

Know the difference between what feels wrong and what feels uncomfortable

Here I was, asking people to quit their jobs and promising to help them build their new career when I never knew how long the company would leave me in place to help fulfill that promise. When I could no longer stand to sit across from somebody in an interview and look them in the eye and make that promise, I knew it was time to move on.

I can't keep doing this. The fun had gone out of it.

I was burned out. If you can't get up every morning and look forward to going to work, you are in the wrong job. I felt like a machine spouting the same spiel every day. Now that I'd gotten a look behind the curtain at this company's management style, I didn't like the way it operated. Management demanded that I burn and churn new sales agents out. The executives didn't care one iota about the long-term negative effects the constant moves would have on my family and me. I was having serious second thoughts about this outfit.

The next week came rumors of another major change within the company's leadership. I sat down with my wife that evening to discuss the latest scuttlebutt. By the end of our talk, we both agreed that we had had enough of this insurance business.

We decided to move to Montana and start all over. My parents invited us to move in with them in Baker, population 3,500 in eastern Montana, until we could get on our feet. The closest city offering more opportunities beyond the oil industry or ranching was Billings, a four-hour drive, which I made frequently to apply for jobs.

While waiting on something to open up, I started driving a truck and trailer rig hauling gravel 160 miles roundtrip, three times a day. There was no heat or air in the truck and no radio. I was working 10-hour days with nobody to talk to. Keep in mind I had just left a job where I had conversations with people all day long. Now I found myself getting to know the habits of the same cows that I saw six times each day along the same highway. When I reached the point where I was having conversations with the cows and waving at them, I told Shirley, "I've got to do something else, and quickly."

We drove up to Billings and were walking through the local mall when I noticed a "Help Wanted" sign in the window of a shop that sold men's clothing. I knew nothing about men's fashion, but I loved sales and figured selling suits couldn't be that hard.

I got hired on the spot, but almost immediately got my hands slapped for wandering the mall in search of potential customers when it was dead inside the store. My manager said he'd gotten a complaint from the mall management. "Why can't I go out in front of the store and drum up business?" I asked, used to being on the hunt for prospects instead of waiting for them to come to me.

"That's the rule," he said.

Well, there's only so much dusting you can do to pass the time in retail sales when we didn't have customers, so I asked to re-do the window displays.

While I was out in the mall, surveying my new window arrangement, a couple walked by and admired the suits I had on display. We struck up a conversation. I quickly realized that his wife would be the determining factor about exactly what and how much they would buy. I put together a whole rack of clothes for her to review. By the time I was finished she bought four new suits along with belts, ties, and undershirts for her husband.

"Have you always been in sales?" the husband asked, looking pleased.

"For a while," I said. "I used to be in the insurance business."

"That's what I do," he said.

I briefly explained that I had gotten frustrated, and I'd left the business. When he asked why, I told him about the company constantly moving us around and not having an opportunity to develop relationships and a clientele.

"I know that company. We take the opposite approach," said the man, handing me his card. It read: Assistant Manager with Banker's Life. "We're all about building relationships. Could I come by your house and talk with you and your wife about it?"

For a second time, I had to do a sales job on Shirley. "I thought you said you were burned out on selling insurance," she said. "Now you are thinking about jumping right back into the frying pan?"

"When I first got into this business, I thought I'd be able to form relationships and build a long-term agency," I said. "But you know that's not at all what we got, so I think I owe it to us to at least give it one more look. I want to hear what this guy has to say."

I signed on the next day and became a health, accident, and life insurance salesman for Banker's Life.

That moment in the mayor of Indianapolis' office affirmed to me something that I'd been feeling for a while: There is a big difference between sales as a job and sales as a career, and it all boils down to relationships. Sales as a job is merely something you do to make money. Sales as a career, the way I envisioned it, only happens when you care about the people you are interacting with, and you genuinely love what you do.

President Theodore Roosevelt once said, "People don't care how much you know until they know how much you care." Once I joined a company that bought into that philosophy, I knew I'd found the perfect fit for me.

Knock-Knock Moments

- Find a genuine way to connect with a prospect.
- There are a lot of ways to approach sales, and you've got to find the right path for you.
- A long-term, satisfying career in sales requires relationship-building.

Chapter Six

The Golden Rules
of Prospecting

"Keep your sales pipeline full by prospecting continuously. Always have more people to see than you have time to see them."

– Brian Tracy

I will let you in on a little secret about selling. The best people in sales know this truth: Only about 20 percent of your time is actually spent selling.

Shocked? If you want to be successful in sales, the lion's share of your time will be spent on prospecting and the remainder on administrative details like paperwork. You are only selling part-time, because you are not always in front of somebody or having direct contact with a potential client on the phone or virtually.

But to be successful, you need to prospect all the time.

When I looked at my scorecard, out of a 50-hour week I might have only been in front of prospects presenting for eight hours or so. The rest of my time was spent filling my funnel.

Keeping your pipeline full requires always keeping an eye open for new clients. The salespeople who not only succeed but thrive are the ones with the best prospecting skills.

In my new company, we were asked to fill a booklet with of the names of people we thought could possibly be clients. You had to come up with 100 names with contact information of people who would be good clients for the types of products that we would be selling. Then your manager helped you sort through this list to see who your hot prospects were, who you should check with in the near future, and who went on the backburner.

Your prospects may come from a variety of sources—referrals, internet research, personal observations, cold calls, and more. No matter what the source, feed all these names through the funnel in order to weed out the ones that you need to postpone contacting for whatever reason, those who are not a good fit right now, those you need to contact right away, and those you need to call back or follow up with later.

When you fill your own funnel with prospects you have generated, your closing ratio goes way up. It doesn't matter what you are selling. If you rely just on buying third-party leads, that means you are relying on someone else to make that judgment call and cede the opportunity to sort out prospects. In doing so, I can guarantee that your closing ratio will go down. But at times you may need to do both to generate enough prospects to keep you busy. Then make the most out of it. There is no such thing as a bad lead. Take those third-party leads and use the techniques we have discussed to generate good prospects on the way to that lead, around that lead, and get referrals or recommendations from that lead. But by all means keep filling that funnel every day with possible new prospects.

Because I thought of prospecting like a funneling process, I eventually came up with my own version of a visual funnel that I used to teach my salespeople that my sales team called a "Dunnel"—**D**oug's **Funnel**. I recommend you do the same.

Sometimes I'd encounter salespeople who claimed they didn't understand the funnel concept. They didn't want to go through the exercise of putting down their prospects or they'd claim that they didn't want to review them with their training manager, out of concern that the manager or some other salesperson might steal them. These were just excuses or crutches holding them up from succeeding. Every single one of them either didn't get hired in the first place or washed out quickly, because they ran out of prospects to call.

I learned to recognize the ones who were like eaglets sitting in the nest, waiting for you to feed them leads. Eagles will eventually remove the feathers that make the nest a little too comfortable and, if need be, will force the eaglets out. That eaglet either learns to hunt very early and make it on their own, or they die. Salespeople fly or die as well. Football was a contact sport that I loved, and sales is, too. You have to have an appetite for it. Print out the slogan "PROSPECT OR DIE" and place it on the dash of your car or by your computer screen so you can see it at all times.

Don't let familiarity breed contempt—or neglect

I was doubly motivated to get out there and sell. Why? Because growing up in a town in Montana where the oil fields and ranching were the main occupations, I'd seen more than my share of accidents, diseases, or deaths that took out the family breadwinner or caused the family a huge financial hardship. I understood how what I was selling—accident, health, and life insurance policies—could make all the difference for a family in such a crisis.

One of my peers came dragging into the office one afternoon. "Why the long face?" I asked.

"I went to my cousin's funeral yesterday, and his widow came up to me and asked, 'Why didn't you ever talk to us about buying a life insurance policy?'" he said. "My cousin was a rancher with three little kids. I didn't have an answer for her, Doug."

I made a vow right then and there that I never, ever wanted to experience that same thing. The worst thing I could imagine would be attending the funeral of a close friend, and his wife comes up and says, "You sell life and accident insurance to complete strangers. Why didn't you ever bother to come over and talk to us?"

Regardless of what you are selling, you owe it to everybody you know to tell them what you do for a living at least once. Because I sell something that most people don't want to think about, I made it a point to tell relatives and close friends, "Look, I need to bring up what I sell and what service I provide families to you at least one time. If you want to know more, then I'm happy to speak with you about it and offer my best advice for your situation. And if you aren't interested, I'll never bring it up again." You have now put the ball in their court.

I never wanted to be that guy at social events and family gatherings that people avoided for fear of being pitched a product or a service. By broaching the topic outside of such an event one time, my conscience was clear because I'd communicated that I felt that I had something they and their family might need but without being a jerk and a pest about it every time I saw them.

Still, you may be like me and have occasions when you fall asleep at the wheel. I needed to wear suits and dress shirts most days for work. We lived in one town for several years, and I had a pleasant relationship with the older lady who ran the local dry cleaner. We laughed and joked every time I dropped off or picked up my dry cleaning.

Finally, it occurred to me that I'd never once bothered to tell her what I did for a living. "That lady should be in my prospect book," I said to myself. The very next time I dropped of my dry cleaning, I told her that I sold life and health insurance for a living.

"Oh, Doug, I wish you would have told me sooner," she said. "I just met with an agent last week and bought a policy."

I had another Knock-Knock Moment one Thursday evening when I'd gotten up from dinner with my family to drive an hour away to an appointment with a new prospect. As I got in my car to leave, a car pulled up at my neighbor's house across the street. I recognized the man who got out as a competitor of mine.

All the way to my appointment, I was chastising myself for never bothering to walk across the street and offer to speak to my neighbor about his insurance needs.

That Saturday, I was out doing yardwork and saw my neighbor. I walked over and gave him my elevator speech about what I sold.

"That's ironic," he said. "I just bought policies for my wife and me earlier this week."

I walked back across the street, knowing I'd driven an hour each way to see a stranger when I'd never bothered to cross the street.

I realized from these two episodes that I needed to include "personal observation" into my prospecting sources and have ever since.

You can be the best salesperson in the world, but if you don't have anybody to go see, or refuse to tell people what you do, guess what? You are a secret agent.

Knock-Knock Moments

- Everybody is a prospect.
- Let the funnel sort out who your hottest prospects are and focus on them first.
- Open your mouth. Tell people what you do.
- Don't be a secret agent.

Chapter Seven

Don't Be A Secret Agent

"Whether you think you can or whether you think you can't, you're right!"

– Henry Ford

When you are in sales or if sales is part of your job, you have to get in the habit of letting people know what services or products you have to offer. Because much more of your time will be spent prospecting for future clients than on presenting and/or selling prospects, you've got to become your own marketing department.

You may be taught traditional marketing methods by your employer on how to generate leads such as using direct mailers, advertising ads, flyers, radio ads, social media, and more. While these methods work, each tactic means you are marketing yourself to complete strangers. These potential customers have not seen your name before, don't recognize your face, have never heard you speak, nor do they know anyone who knows you.

If you sit back and hope that some of them will respond to you, I guarantee one thing: You'll never reach your potential in sales. The real power lies in your willingness to open your mouth and sell yourself.

Sell yourself where your feet are

I never had the personality to sit back and wait for prospects to come to me. I quickly learned how to market where my feet are. While I continue to use some of the traditional marketing techniques, I have found there is an easier way to generate leads that typically turn out to be even better leads. Wherever you are is the best place you can sell.

Let me give you an example of how this works. I was driving to a home to visit with a woman who had responded to one of our direct mailing campaigns and had requested more information. Now I only had this one lead, and it was quite a trip out to where she lives, so I started looking for possible customers along the way.

Since I was calling on seniors, it was a little easier to profile possible clients. I saw a woman working in her front yard and got out to talk to her.

I had the lead card in my hand, introduced myself, and asked her if she knew Margaret and where Oak Street was. Once she saw I was not there to sell her, she opened right up and started telling me where Oak Street was and about what time Margaret got home each day from baby-sitting her grandson.

I then used a 'Columbo' technique—like the detective played by Peter Falk on the old television show by that name. I thanked her for the information and turned to leave, paused and turned around, and asked, "By the way, are you happy with your current Medicare coverage, or could I answer any questions for you while I am here?"

She said, "Why, as a matter of fact, I do have some questions." Then she invited me into the house. I signed up both her and her husband that day, and the lead on the prospect named Margaret ended up being a dead end.

Talk about what you do

A friend of mine always says, "You have to tell people how to think about you." If you are excited that you have taken on a new career in sales, then TELL PEOPLE! When you tell people what you do and how you can help serve them or provide something that they want, then they tell others.

People like to buy from people they know, or from someone recommended by a trusted friend or colleague. That's why finding the circle of influence in your community is so critical. These super-spreaders help you get the word out.

Craft a good elevator speech

One of the first things you need to do is develop an elevator pitch: a short and sweet summary that quickly and simply defines your profession, product, service, organization, and its value proposition. In other words, who you are, what you do, and who you do it for.

Think about the brief moment when you are on an elevator as all the time you have to deliver that information. Your pitch should be thirty to sixty seconds.

You'd be surprised at how many people don't bother to think through their elevator pitch. They ramble and leave the other person sorry that they asked a question. The other day I met someone who had just moved to town, and after I gave him my elevator speech, I asked what he did for a living. He talked for a full five minutes, and he had lost me in the first 30 seconds.

When he finally stopped talking, I still wasn't quite sure what his job entailed. My wife Shirley and I walked away, and I asked, "Did you understand what he does for a living?"

She said, "No."

I was relieved that it wasn't just me.

Being long-winded or confusing in your pitch guarantees that not only will your listener walk away baffled, but your chances of getting referrals are nil.

Your pitch is designed to pique the listener's curiosity and leave them wanting to know more. If you get a question or a request for more information, you know you have their attention. If your conversation in those few seconds is interesting it will either continue, or end in exchange of business cards, contact information, or a scheduled meeting.

If you asked someone what they do, and they answer, "I am an insurance agent," the conversation may end right there. They may already feel they know what that person does and dismiss the need to hear any more.

You should be able to explain what you do in some detail, but without using jargon or terminology that pigeonholes you and bores your listener.

A good elevator speech is designed to:

- <u>Tell them who you are.</u> Give your name and title.
- <u>Make them care.</u> What can you do for them or their loved ones?
- <u>Make it a conversation</u>. Make it easy for them to join in the conversation or ask questions.
- <u>Leave them wanting more.</u> Keep it short.
- <u>Have a call to action.</u> If you are trying to generate a lead, ask for it. If you are trying to set an appointment, ask for it.
- <u>Practice.</u> To be natural in pulling off a good, effective elevator speech, you need to practice, practice, practice with a friend or family member. Get feedback. Get comfortable with it.

A good elevator speech is like having a sign around your neck that tells people who you are and what you do. What does your sign say?

You only get to make a first impression once!

Dress the Part

When I started my career in sales, I made radical changes to my appearance. I shaved off my shaggy goatee and cut my long hair and stopped wearing my earring. I knew that look wasn't going to fly in conservative east Texas when I was calling on small business owners, mayors, and judges. You may need to make adjustments, too, depending on your target audience.

All the research shows that you have six seconds before that person forms an opinion of you. Six seconds! Make sure you are dressing for the part everywhere you go, or whether you are working from home and conducting video meetings.

You are coding yourself for non-verbal communication, and you are making it either easier for prospects to know who you are, or you are creating unnecessary static in the communication channel.

With more and more business being conducted online and in video meetings and webinars, be especially aware of what's going on in the background. Maybe something's hanging on the wall that you don't want the whole world to see. Family and pets may interrupt. Be mindful of how your environment looks and whether it's even wise to conduct a video call from that location.

Are you dressed properly? How are you lit? Move a lamp behind the screen so that you are lit in soft, daylight temperature bulbs. Make sure the background behind you is uncluttered. Your rec room may be quiet, but the beer keg in front of the dart board behind you probably doesn't build confidence.

In today's environment, I now ask all new hires whether they are set up at home to be able to conduct business and prospect if they need to.

Your appearance is critical to your business. In sales, your first impression comes from your personal appearance, your approach, your introduction, and how you make that person in front of you feel in those first six seconds.

Every sales job and every salesperson is in some way different. As such, there's no official rulebook for sales job attire. Consult with your employer right off the bat—know your company's dress code inside out. Don't worry about looking too uptight or stuffy in a suit. Dressing up shows your prospects that you respect them and their time.

But this does not mean every salesperson needs to be in business attire for all appointments. Dress for your audience. A SnapOn Tool salesperson wears what makes the mechanics being called upon comfortable, but yet needs to project a sense of professionalism.

Your first impression may be via email, social media, or a LinkedIn introduction. Don't send out long emails to introduce yourself or your intent. If you don't get my attention with the subject line or the first sentence, or you misspell my name, I hit delete. Take the time to Google and find out something about your prospect and whether they go by Robert or Bobby, or Cynthia or Cindy.

It's the same thought as the elevator speech whether the first contact is by phone, social media, email, or a webinar. You've got to be prepared and make a great first impression.

Details count

If it's an in-person appointment, keep your vehicle clean and orderly. Never park in a driveway or in front of a mailbox. If your vehicle leaks oil, park far away from your prospect's home or place of business. More than once I've gotten a call from a prospect who withdrew their business because the agent's vehicle left an oil stain. That lack of attention to detail can cost you dearly.

Confidence in you is built when people believe you can do what you say and then give you the opportunity to prove yourself.

Give a great greeting and a strong smile. People do business with the people they like and trust.

Always have a business card on you. Be able to whip that business card out in the blink of an eye. I have seen more first impressions spoiled by someone fumbling for five minutes trying to find their business card in their purse or pockets. When that happens, the business card is usually bent or dirty to boot.

Have a pen on you at all times. I have written good prospects' names and contact information on the back of my cards, receipts, or torn corners of a handy piece of paper. You make them feel important by writing their name and contact info down. And if you take their information down, do something with it soon. If you wait even a week, you may as well have never met them. The hot lead has lost its steam.

Your first impression should project that you are an expert on the subject matter you have come to discuss and not a distraction.

Networking

Raise your hand if you belong to an association, religious group, alumni group, charity, group of hobbyists, book club, or professional organization. We all do. Great. This means you have a built-in source of leads already. This is the perfect place to talk about yourself, what you do, and ask for referrals.

When networking, your power comes from building those relationships. They will care when they see how much you care. When attending these meetings, network with results in mind so you're not wasting your time or theirs.

Networking makes you <u>the</u> expert they call when the product you sell or the service you offer is needed from someone they are talking to.

Commit by putting those events on your calendar. Be a regular attendee and give to the group.

Let me give an example of how important those last four words are.

I had been invited to speak at an insurance association's annual meeting that was made up of all women in the Dallas/Fort Worth market. Upon arriving, they immediately hit me up to buy a $20 ticket for the door prize they had been raffling off for the past 12 months. I felt a little peer pressure to buy a ticket, but did so. At the conclusion of my speech, I sat back in my chair at the head table, and they started drawing names out for all the prizes they had offered in this annual fundraiser. They then did a drum-roll for the grand prize, which was an all-expenses-paid, 10-day Caribbean cruise.

I was shocked to hear my name called, but apparently not as shocked as they were. You see, they had been selling tickets to all of their members for the past year, and the only man in attendance that day had just won <u>their</u> grand prize. Normally, I would have donated the prize back to the group, but my 25th wedding anniversary was coming up, and this prize was going home with me. At one point when I was leaving, I felt I might need a bodyguard. Even though I had spoken to this group at least once a year, that was my last invitation. There went my opportunity for net-working with that association again.

Choose wisely when it comes to which event you should attend. Make sure the audience is the right one for you.

Family and friends

Your family and friends are great resources to assist you in moving your business forward. Practice your elevator speech on them.

The people who are close to you each have a network of people, and they can be your biggest advocates. Talk to them. You owe it to them and to yourself. Ask them who they know that might have a need for the products or services you sell.

Again, don't be a secret agent.

Knock-Knock Moments

- Pick your time and place to talk about what you do, but don't miss opportunities.
- Pay attention to the small things. You only make a first impression once.
- Develop a good elevator pitch and use it daily.
- Be a giver, or you might shoot yourself in the foot.

Chapter Eight

The Key Ingredient of Super-charged Sales: Positive Mental Attitude

"Like success, failure is many things to many people. With Positive Mental Attitude, failure is a learning experience, a rung on the ladder, a plateau at which to get your thoughts in order and prepare to try again."

—W. Clement Stone

Warning: When you decide to make your career in sales, be prepared to get a lot of blowback. By the very nature of the sales process, you are going to experience a lot of rejection on a daily basis. At any step along the way—from your initial knock, knock on the door to your close—you may get shutdown. Get used to hearing NO a lot.

On top of that, some folks have had a bad experience with salespeople. That stereotype of the pushy salesperson may be something else you'll have to deal with at times. But some of the biggest naysayers may be people you wouldn't expect to be negative: your significant other, your family, and even your closest friends.

Why am I telling you all of this? Because there's an antidote to all the rejection and negativity you are bound to encounter in sales. Where can you find the cure? Right between your ears—in your mind. If you can keep your thoughts focused on the positive, you'll find much greater success. Not only in sales, but in life as well.

I am grateful that my instructor in insurance school drilled the importance of a positive mental attitude into us. Then it was reinforced by my early training—each morning in our sales meeting, at noon when we touched base again, and then at the end of the day before we went home. I learned about authors like Zig Ziglar, W. Clement Stone, and Earl Nightingale, who wrote about positive mental attitude.

I'd never been much of a reader prior to getting into sales, but I devoured these books. Every page was a WOW!

I could read a chapter at night, and I could put what I'd learned into use the following day. It was proven practical knowledge and principles. The more embedded these positive sayings and ideas became in my mind, and the more I applied them on a daily basis in my life, the more I could see the direct result in my bank account.

I got so excited about the impact of these authors' books. Studying their books made me better. I made a habit of writing down quotes that resonated with me and sticking them on the dashboard of my car. That way, even if I had a sales call that went badly, I'd have something positive to remind me to keep going as soon as I got back in my car. Filling my mind with affirmations helped me go home at the end of the day, no matter my results, and still feel successful and confident that I'd done my best that day.

At times seemingly everybody is telling you NO, so you need positive upbeat messages to keep you going. Fortunately, my wife Shirley was behind me 100 percent. At least I didn't have to worry about being undermined on the home front like some of my colleagues experienced.

That wasn't the case with my father or some other members of my family. Dad didn't say much, but he was deeply disappointed that I didn't get my engineering degree and go into the oil business alongside him. I was ten years into my career in sales and a regional manager before he ever acknowledged any of my success in sales.

I am so grateful that that first company where I got my sales training so heavily emphasized self-help books that dealt with a positive mindset. Although by nature I have always been pretty happy-go-lucky, nobody when I was growing up other than my football and basketball coaches had ever talked about the importance of focusing on the positive in order to achieve your goals. Getting that foundation under me helped give me a solid launching pad for my sales career.

Getting your head in the game

Why is your mindset so important? Without a positive attitude, I can guarantee that somewhere in the sales process something will go off-track. Your potential customer can sense your lack of confidence, your frustration, your insincerity, your desperation, or your lack of enthusiasm for the product or service you are selling. You cannot afford to make a single phone call, to send an email, to join a virtual meeting, or to make an in-person sales call if you are in a funk. People will pick up on your negative energy in a heartbeat.

That's the reason that, to this day—my fifth decade in sales—I still review what went well and what didn't after every point of communication. If something wasn't the best, I think about how I can improve and reach out for advice if I need it. Then I move on. I don't dwell on mistakes or strikeouts and endlessly ruminate over them.

So how do you shake it off when you blow it or are just having a bad day? Each person needs to find what works for them. I almost always have what I call a steering wheel review after a sales call to go over what went well and what didn't and why. But after that review, I make myself think about the next item on my agenda and mentally shake it off. When I was making cold calls door-to-door, sometimes I'd go into the men's room at a gas station and give myself a pep talk. I'd do jumping jacks and get my blood pumping, so that when I approached the next prospect I'd have enthusiasm and good energy. I'd play my favorite radio station on the ride between appointments. Music can change your mood.

What I saw as I was training more and more new agents was that each individual has to have a hunger, a burning desire to make this work. You can't transfer or train that into somebody. They have to want it for themselves.

I'll never forget this one agent-in-training. He was handsome, well spoken, passed all the tests, and memorized the presentations. I took him on ride-alongs, and he really seemed to get it. That is until the time came for me to be the silent partner and observe him making the pitch.

He would freeze. I'd try to do a soft handoff, but he couldn't get over the mental hurdle and pick up the ball and run with it. Finally, I told him, "Jerry, we are going into that bank and I am not going to say a word. This one is all yours."

We went up to the receptionist, and he clammed up. She looked at him and then at me and back at him. Dead silence. Finally, I said, "Jerry, do you have something you want to say to this lady?"

He could not get a single word out of his mouth. I apologized to her, and when we got out on the sidewalk I said, "We can work on skills, but what I can't change is your desire to make this work. You can either keep going and break through this block, or you can go home. But we can't keep doing this."

He quit that day. I have no idea what the negative voice was that he had in his head, but he couldn't silence it enough to allow him to apply all the skills he'd learned and actually sell.

Some people appear to be born with a negative outlook on life. If you know you are one of those people, do yourself a favor and do not go into sales.

I am always surprised by the Negative Neds and Nellies who go into sales. You know the type. They rarely smile, they've never had a boss or a job that they liked, and the only game they play regularly is the blame game with a big glass of whine.

With one of my employers that sells supplemental Medicare policies, we had a deal with a big box chain store where our agents could have a booth in the company's stores for a $500 fee for a 10-week term. If they didn't feel like they were getting much traction, they would quickly blame the store location or the placement of their booth within this store before ever taking a self-review or ownership of the results generated.

This one man kept calling us a few weeks into his contract, demanding his money back.

I headed to this store to see what was going on. I'm in the age range of his prime customer, so I figured I'd watch him work and be able to pinpoint the problem in his sales pitch. I walked by his booth seven times. He never once looked up from the novel he was engrossed in.

Finally, I walked up and said, "Hey, what are you doing here?"

"Excuse me?" he said, looking annoyed that I'd interrupted his reading.

"What are you selling?" I asked.

He told me, and then I said, "Do I look like a senior to you?"

"Well, yes," he stammered, and awkwardly started his pitch.

By this time, I was frustrated, and interrupted him. "I'm from the company that brought you the products you are supposed to be representing in this store, but you never once looked up from your book at any point during the seven times I passed by your booth," I said. "You aren't smiling at anybody or attempting to start a conversation. Instead, you look like you are challenging them to knock that chip off your shoulder. Scoot over a minute."

For the next hour, I ran his booth and showed him how to start several conversations by just looking approachable, friendly, and making eye contact with everyone who walked by.

After I proved my point, I said, "Right now you are acting like a secret agent and waiting for people to challenge you to a conversation. No wonder you aren't getting any sales. If you aren't going to show these people walking right in front of you that you are approachable and open for business, then you need to go do something else."

"Pretend that every single person you meet has a sign around his or her neck that says, 'make me feel important.' Not only will you succeed in sales, you will succeed in life."

– Mary Kay Ash

The danger of snap judgment

When I'd been promoted to regional sales manager in eastern Montana, the vice president of the company called me from the home office in Chicago and said, "Doug, I need a favor. There's a guy in my hometown in Butte, who I went to high school with, and I need you to hire him. He got hurt on the job in the copper mine, and he needs this job badly."

"What about the aptitude tests and interview process?" I asked. "Are you telling me you want him hired no matter what?"

"Well, I guess that's exactly what I am saying, Doug," he said, adding, "and keep this between you and me. Nobody else in the company is to know."

It was a three-hour drive for me to go meet this fellow. I took another agent with me, so we could work our way down there and work our way back. We interviewed him at a pizza shop in Butte, Montana. He showed up looking slightly disheveled, not dressed quite right, and his hair looked overly greasy. I noticed something yellow in it. At the end of the interview I asked about it, and, flushing red, he said, "I ran out of Brylcreem and used a little bit of butter today."

I thought, *No way will this guy make it through the testing process.*

As soon as we got back in the car for the drive back to Billings, my colleague said, "You aren't going to bring him on, are you?"

"Let's see how he does in the testing," I said, figuring that he'd bomb badly, and I'd be saved by our company's rule that we could not make any exceptions to the testing process.

To my shock, he scored pretty well. I was on the hook now. I had to hire him. I called him up and told him I needed to come by and have a second interview. "Where do you want to meet?" I asked.

"Please come by my house," he said, and gave me the address.

When I arrived, Daniel was looking out the window of something I can only describe as a shack. He greeted me at the front door, shaking my hand. He was dressed in a suit and tie, and three little girls were sitting on the couch all dressed up in their Sunday best. He introduced me, and his wife came out from the kitchen where she'd just finished baking an apple pie and set it to cool.

"Why don't we sit at the kitchen table so we can take a look at some paperwork?" I suggested. The youngest daughter walked up to me and tugged on my arm.

"Mister, are you the man who is going to give my daddy a job?" she asked, looking at me with wide innocent eyes. I still wasn't certain about hiring him until I saw the hope in her eyes.

"Why, yes," I said. "Yes, I am." In that moment, I vowed to do whatever I had to do to help this man be successful. I ditched my negative attitude over being told that I had to hire him and gave him my very best training and support.

Daniel had hurt his back in the copper mine and had not worked for months, and they had next to no money to their name. So I took him to Goodwill and helped him pick out some more suitable clothes, to the drugstore for some personal care products, and to a barber to get him a haircut. He passed his final insurance tests the next week with flying colors and was now ready to go to work.

Humility helps you see people and meet their needs

I drove back down to Butte to start his field training. We made several sales those first few days, so they now had some money coming their way, but we talked about prospecting and every single aspect of the sales process all week long.

"Don't forget, you can't rely just on our company leads. You need to learn to just sell where your feet are just like we have been doing all week," I said.

Early Sunday morning, after we'd completed that first week of his initial training, my phone rang.

"Doug, I need your help. I've got my first sale, but I don't know how to fill out the application," he said.

"Where are you, Daniel?" I asked, noting the early hour.

"I'm at a truck stop," he said.

"A truck stop? Why did you go there?"

"I figured I might find some drivers who needed health and accident insurance, so I came over here around 4 am, figuring they might be stopped for breakfast and willing to talk."

"So you've got a truckdriver to write up?" I asked.

"No, it's a working lady. She was sitting at the counter in the coffee shop here, and I started talking to her. I asked her what kind of work she did. Then she explained to me that she is a lady of the evening, and I'm not quite sure how to put that occupation on the app."

I couldn't let him fail to get his first solo sale, and I was shocked by the grit and determination he demonstrated to get it. He had followed my advice to the letter and certainly was talking and selling where his feet were.

You have to understand that in Butte, Montana, this was a legal profession, but not in Chicago, where headquarters were. We ended up agreeing to put her occupation down as a "self-employed salesperson".

That man went on to become one of the best salespeople in the entire four-state region. Within a year, he bought a new Cadillac and finished the repairs on his home.

And this was a guy that I didn't want to hire when I first met him and that nobody else in our company believed in either. The difference-maker for him was that he kept a positive attitude no matter what circumstance he was facing. I've never met anyone more capable of letting rejection roll off his back than Daniel. Nothing slowed him down, and he never allowed anything to get him down. He just needed a chance.

"Positive thinking will let you do everything better than negative thinking will."

– Zig Ziglar

In fact, when I got promoted and moved out of state, he took over as district manager for that part of Montana, moved to Billings, and built a new home. On that positive note, I'll end this chapter.

Knock-Knock Moments

- Expect adversity and naysayers.
- Have strategies to delete negative thoughts and shake off sales appointments that go south.
- Never underestimate the power of a positive attitude.

Chapter Nine

Winners Never Stop Learning

*"If you are not willing to learn, no one can
help you. If you are determined to learn,
no one can stop you."*

– Zig Ziglar

The people who thrive in sales are those who put in the work to stay on top of the current trends in their respective industries. The worst thing you can do is to get in a rut, doing the same old same old.

**"Even if you are on the right track, you'll get run over
if you just sit there."**

– Will Rogers

Nothing kills your sales career faster than being unwilling to learn and grow. Technology is always changing. The best forms of communication for the particular customer you want to reach are always changing. Your products or services may change. Sales techniques change.

In more than forty years in my sales career in the insurance industry, I've seen a world of change. Experience is invaluable, but only if you keep adding product/service knowledge and sales skills. I ask new agents, "Ten years from now are you going to have ten years of experience or one year of experience ten times?"

Why do I ask that question? Because far too many people go through sales training and rely solely on that initial training. They expect that first round of training to get them by forever. They expect to be spoon-fed anything of value, and they expect to be successful with a limited formula. It doesn't work that way. To really get good at something, you've got to keep investing in yourself and strive to keep learning.

In one sense, it's easier than ever to educate yourself on sales. We have Podcasts; audio, print and e-books from authors like Seth Godin, Brian Tracy, and Jeffrey Gitomer; YouTube videos; TedTalks; webinars; and much more. But the one ingredient I see in short supply is in-person mentoring: Getting to ride-along with someone, watch a sales veteran in action, and then do it yourself and get feedback. That's not common anymore. That's why I wrote this book: to take you on a ride-along and share what I've learned.

You have to really want help and seek out good mentors who can help you get better. Then practice your elevator speech and sales presentation with your family and close friends over and over. Get their honest feedback and adjust accordingly.

Knowledge builds Confidence

Confidence builds Enthusiasm

Enthusiasm makes the Sale

Nothing is more expensive than a missed opportunity

I started in a company where we only made cold calls, but later worked for a company where agents made cold calls but were also furnished with leads. In a manager's role with that company, my job every Monday meeting was to hand out company leads that had just come in. But we still taught agents to supplement those leads by making cold calls on the way there, on each side of this lead, and on the way home. But some agents continually tried to cut the process short and to make a living just on the leads alone.

I had one agent who was always complaining that his leads were no good. So I decided to take him out one day to show him that it wasn't the quality of the leads that was holding him back. Once we got into the neighborhood, I would pull over when I saw a senior working in the yard and walk up and ask for directions to the lead I had in my hand. Then I asked, "By the way, do you know the person we are trying to locate?"

All of a sudden, the senior relaxed, because we were not trying to sell them. Three times in a row that day, we got invited into the home on the spot and made a sale in that household. When we finally got out to the lead's house, she turned us down.

We got back in the car, and I said, "Yep, you're right. The lead is no good."

He got the point.

You can learn by watching sales pros in other industries, too. When I get sales calls, I listen to see if there is anything I can pick up. If you are in sales, opportunities abound for you to see what works and what doesn't.

Recently the driver for Schwan Home Service knocked on my door. "I happened to be delivering frozen fresh foods to your neighbors, the Taylors, and thought I'd stop by to see if you needed anything while I was here," he said, showing me a catalogue with some of their offerings.

He was using the same pitch I have implemented for forty-some-odd years—using leads to get you in the neighborhood and then making cold calls. I ended up becoming a customer, not because I needed his ice cream, but because he was a good salesman. It was a great reminder from another industry—home food delivery—of what had always worked for me.

The key is a desire to get better and having your antennae up all the time.

For example, in the life and accident insurance industry we relied on getting referrals from our customers. But in my current Medicare supplemental insurance business, the government has stepped in with regulations that have stopped us from asking a senior for a referral's name and phone number. Your existing customer has to have the referral contact you directly themselves. You cannot reach out to this new referral directly. Plus, due to new regulations, we are not allowed to cold call seniors, looking for potential clients.

Because our product offerings can be confusing and need to be tailored to an individual's needs, our sales process called for mostly face-to-face meetings. That has meant agents have to get more creative and make contact with the administrator of a place where seniors live or congregate and get permission to be on-site with a kiosk, or have a booth/kiosk inside a big-box store, grocery store, or pharmacy that attracts a lot of seniors. Or our sales process requires spending a good amount of money on direct-mail advertising.

Now with the pandemic, the opportunities for face-to-face meetings are far more limited than ever. Complicating matters is the fact that we are working with a target population that often isn't adept with technology. The challenges are pretty daunting, but we are working hard to figure out the best ways to connect with our potential clients. We looked at best practices of other industries and have begun to incorporate those ideas. We had to cancel our upcoming in-person conference with our agents, which is an annual highlight for most of us. Instead, we reached out directly and fielded a lot of questions from our agents and discussed new options over endless Zoom meetings.

The result? We needed to learn and do things differently to get over the roadblocks presented to us in March and April 2020 in the form of a pandemic. With many of our potential clients quarantined in their homes, they were much easier to reach. So we started training agents on how to sell over the phone better and how to host mini-webinars with potential clients, so they can show them all the features of the plans available to them via their computers. Our willingness to learn and do things differently increased our sales by 12% for the month of April 2020, when other businesses were shut down.

That is pretty powerful evidence that when you are willing to learn something new and then pivot using that knowledge, you can still thrive. Even under the toughest circumstances.

Don't get so caught up on the new that you forget the basics

A few years ago, an agent asked me if we had ever tried a certain technique, and I replied, "We used to do that all the time, and it worked really well."

"Sounds great. So why did you quit?" he asked.

His question stopped me in my tracks. It was a great reminder that sometimes we get so focused on the latest, greatest technology or technique that we forget the tried-and-true basics that got us to where we are in the first place. "I guess I just forgot to keep doing it," I said. "You are absolutely right. Time for us to go back to it."

Continually expanding your knowledge has one risk: Sometimes you gain so much knowledge that you forget the basics.

Within six months of being with Bankers as an agent, I was out-producing all of the veterans in this office month after month. Before I arrived on the scene the two top-performers, Paul and Bud, had jockeyed for the #1 spot each month for more than twenty years.

My goal was to be named Top Agent of the Month from that point on. I became friendly with the secretary in the office, and the Friday night before the first Monday of the month she would let me know who was in the lead. Because of this inside information, many a Saturday and Sunday night at the end of the month I'd be out making sales calls to be certain I'd beat them Monday morning.

Bud was getting fed up with this new kid beating him each month. One of those Monday meetings, Bud didn't show up downstairs in the meeting room. During a break, I asked the secretary, "Where's Bud?"

"He is going door-to-door down the street," she said. "He asked me how many more apps he needed to beat you."

Toward the end of the meeting Bud came down the stairs, grinning. He had beaten me by one sale.

Sideline your pride

About this same time, the assistant manager who had hired me out of the men's clothing store took another position with a competitor. His management position with our company became available. So I threw my hat in the ring. Paul had been around for years. He was the old-timer, but all of a sudden, he decided that he wanted to be an assistant manager and put his hat in the ring as well.

The boss hired me.

I heard through the grapevine that Paul was upset with me. We had a company rule that a manager had to work in the field with every agent in our office at least once every six months to spot-check them. No matter how long they'd been with the company. For the past five months Paul's production had not been good, and certainly was not up to his average numbers each month.

After three months in my new management position, I called him in Bozeman and asked to meet him in a café. He had been coming to our monthly meetings, but continued to give me the cold shoulder.

I brought his production reports to our meeting and showed him how his numbers had been falling off and asked him if he knew why. He just glared at me. Finally, I said, "Paul, let's just go to work. Let's make some calls."

He agreed but insisted on taking his car, which was an old Datsun. Paul was even bigger than me and twice my age, and we were shoulder-to-shoulder in this small car, driving through prairie on a gravel road in western Montana where he said he had an appointment.

I could practically feel the steam coming off of him. *He's going to bury me out here in the back hills of Montana*, I thought.

We finally got to the first appointment. He made the presentation and asked the customer to buy and then he just kept talking. The customer never really had a chance to respond. He did the same thing on the next two calls. You are supposed to close and stay closed, leaving the ball squarely in the customer's court.

We stopped for lunch, and I brought up this issue. "Paul, I'd been looking forward to doing a ride-along with you, because I know I have so much to learn from you," I said. "You gave a great presentation. But I noticed when you close, you're not giving the customer an opportunity to buy. You keep talking right through the close."

Did I mention he was a big guy? He sat there for what seemed like an eternity.

Finally, he said, "You know what? You may have something there. I had already been aware that my numbers were slipping. I've been trying even harder to correct that. But apparently, I have been pressuring people to the point that I'm now working outside of the process."

I said, "Yep, you bail them out when you start talking again during the close."

We agreed that he'd take the next call and try to correct this. It was married students in university housing. The couple had two little kids in diapers, running around the table and playing. Paul got to the close and asked, "In your opinion, which option is the best plan for you? Option A or Option B?"

Dead silence. Nobody was talking. This silence went on forever. It got so quiet even the toddlers stopped running around to look at the adults. The husband was studying the paperwork, and the wife looked at us and then looked at him.

Finally, she said to her husband, "So?"

"We lost!" he cried, and jumped up from the table. "You made us lose. They just closed us. They used the assumed close. That's what I did all the time when I sold encyclopedias for six months."

No prospect had ever used the terminology we use as salespeople in a presentation. We sat there with our mouths gaping open for a minute and then Paul calmly said, "Did I understand correctly, was that Option B you wanted to go with?"

I could barely contain my laughter. We became best friends at that moment. He started telling me his sales secrets. He later confessed, "They had asked me to be a manager a dozen times, and I turned them down. At my age I don't have the energy for it. From what I've seen with you, Doug, they made the right choice. Plus, Bud and I no longer have to compete with you each month."

"Always walk through life as if you have something new to
learn and you will."

—Vernon Howard

Knock-Knock Moments

- Change or die. Decide to keep growing in your profession.
- Ten years from now, are you going to have ten years of experience or one year of experience ten times?
- Look to other industries and study others' sales processes and techniques.
- Everybody serves as an example—either a bad one or a good one.
- Be open to learning from someone less experienced than you and someone with more experience than you.

Chapter Ten

Teaching Moments

"I touch the future. I teach."

– Christa McAuliffe

On a January winter morning in eastern Montana, I was driving sixty miles across the frozen prairie to a large ranch that bordered the North Dakota Badlands for a 9:00 am appointment with a rancher and his family to discuss their health and life insurance needs. This was back in the days before cell phones or GPS systems, so on these winding gravel roads all you had to rely on were the directions you wrote down when setting up the appointment.

In this part of eastern Montana there were no trees, just small rolling plains of either wheat fields or grazing pastures for cattle. There were no street or road signs, so my directions gave instructions such as: *Turn right at the 25th fence post past the smaller of two rises in the road.*

I finally made it on time to this ranch in the middle of nowhere. I sat at the kitchen table, going over all of their healthcare and life insurance options in great detail with both the rancher and his wife. After taking another hour to complete all of the applications for the couple and their adult children, it was now 12:30 in the afternoon.

Read the signs

The rancher wrote a large check for the annual premiums for all the plans. He placed that check on top of the paperwork we had just completed in the middle of the table. Then he asked, "Doug, would you care to join us for lunch?"

I was concerned about how much of their time I had taken on this snowy morning. I was also aware that his wife had not even started preparing lunch, so I replied, "Thanks a million, but I really need to get started on the long drive back to town."

Then a Knock-Knock Moment of extreme importance occurred right in front of me in what seemed like slow motion. The rancher placed one finger on top of the check he had just written and, as he dragged it off the pile of applications, he said, "Son, if you are not good enough to eat with my family, then you are not good enough to handle my business."

After I could breathe again I took off my coat, sat back down, and asked, "What are we having?"

While his wife prepared lunch, he walked me around his beautiful home, proudly showing me pictures of his great-great-grandparents, who originally started this ranch, while educating me on business etiquette in this part of the county. "Someone out here in the country would have never asked you to sit and share a meal with them unless they really liked and trusted you," he said. "We do not issue that invitation lightly, and neither should you take it lightly."

This valuable lesson helped me tremendously in building client relationships in Big Sky country going forward.

Be generous with your knowledge

The time came to make that sixty-mile drive across snow-covered gravel roads back to town. Keep in mind, there was a three-foot blanket of snow across the countryside. On top of that it had snowed while I was in their house, so the tracks I made on the drive out were now covered by fresh powder. Although they had given me directions for the drive to their house, they had not provided directions for the return trip.

While this may not sound like an issue to some of you, keep in mind a direction to *Turn right at the T in the road* does not compute when you are going back the other direction and can barely see the road you are on.

After what seemed like an eternity, I finally came across a building just off the road with a car and a pickup parked next to it and two horses tied to a fence. The sign on the front read: *Fallon Creek School.* Smoke was rising from the chimney of the potbelly stove, so I deduced that school was in session.

I knocked on the door, and a friendly young woman opened it. She looked surprised and curious to see me standing there dressed in a suit and tie at this time of day. I told her who I was, what I did for a living, and why I was out in these parts. "I am hopelessly lost, and ma'am, I'd be grateful if you could give me directions back to the highway," I said.

She cocked her head to the side, grinned, and said, "I'll be happy to provide you directions on one condition."

"What's that?"

"Give a talk to my class first."

Now it was my turn to be surprised. "Sure," I stammered. "But about what?"

"Your profession," she said. "Tell the class what insurance is and why there is a need for it."

"You've got a deal," I said, and walked up to the front of the classroom. Scanning the room and sizing up my audience, I realized I had a new challenge: how to give a talk that would appeal to the first-graders as well as the eighth-graders in this one-room schoolhouse. I had to find a way to tackle the complicated subject of insurance that was not over the heads of some and over-simplified for others. To buy time to figure out what I was going to say, I decided to find out what they already knew. I started around the room, asking each one what their name was and what they thought insurance was.

The responses and feedback I got were fantastic. The little ones would come out with some wild notion about insurance, and the older students would correct them and explain what they thought it was. After witnessing these exchanges, I understood that these lively discussions were part of how topics were taught in this country school. I then gave an Insurance 101 explanation and spoke about the financial risks that insurance covers. Miss Wilson broke into a wide grin. I had earned my directions.

> **"If there is richness and righteousness in us, then we can make a difference in the lives of others, just as key individuals have influenced the lives of each of us for good and made us richer than we otherwise would have been."**
>
> **– Spencer W. Kimball**

Miss Wilson declared a recess and told the class to go outside and play. As they headed out the door, they each came by one-by-one to thank me for coming by to visit with them. The teacher had written out the directions back to town and thanked me for the great break in their day's routine.

I put on my coat, gloves and overshoes, and stepped outside. These kids were not done with me yet. This one-room schoolhouse sat on top of a small hill, and the children had procured two large sheets of cardboard that they were using as a sled to slide down the hill through the deep snow. A group approached and pestered me to take a ride down the hill with them.

I looked at Miss Wilson, and she nodded that it was okay with her. After the day I had just had, I said, "You bet. Let's go!" They all cheered. Some of the older ones helped me climb onto the sheet of cardboard. Once I was in place there was room for a couple of the little ones, who jumped onboard without asking. The older boys then gave us a shove off that hillside. Apparently, Miss Wilson hadn't covered physics, and that wasn't my area of study either. Due to my size and weight, this homemade sled took off at what felt like 90 mph down the hillside. Kids were screaming and yelling as we bounced all the way down. Once we finally came to a stop, I turned and looked back up the hill. I was shocked when I realized how far we had actually come. The long walk back through deep snow, dragging that homemade toboggan, wasn't easy. When I finally made it to the top of the hill all the kids were laughing, yelling, and screaming, "Let's go again!"

Miss Wilson came to the rescue and said, "Recess is over. Everyone back into school."

I thanked her for the opportunity to talk to the kids and for her directions. Between breaths, I also told her, "I don't think I could have made another trip up that hill."

She smiled and whispered, "I don't think you could have either."

The next day I got a phone message at the office that the rancher wanted to talk to me. I wondered, *What is this about?*

When I got him on the phone, he was laughing up a storm and said, "Doug, you are one quick learner. Two of those kids you agreed to do a talk for and take a slide with down that hill were my kids. Miss Wilson lives with us during the school season, and we heard all about your day at our school. Way to go, young man!"

Not only did I get multiple referrals from the rancher, but I wrote a health policy on Miss Wilson a few weeks later.

Since that accidental teaching opportunity presented itself that day, I have volunteered to talk to children and teens in schools all over the country about:

- what insurance is;
- when you need it and when you don't;
- and what a fantastic career sales can be.

That experience was a wake-up call. From that day forward, I started thinking of myself as more of an educator than as an insurance salesman. For the rest of my career that's the mindset I've had when I'm with a prospect or client, educating them on their current coverage and what other options are available that could reduce that risk; in a public forum as a speaker; or in a school setting bringing real-life education to students.

I wish that more people would volunteer to talk to our children about careers in the trade industry and professions like sales that are likely unfamiliar. Most all discussion at the high school level centers on the need to go to college while many students quietly sit there knowing they will never go down that path and are wondering, "What about me?" You could well be the person who enters that young person's life at just the right time and answers that question for them.

Knock-Knock Moments

- Make sure you understand the business etiquette where you are selling. Keep in mind that there can be unspoken rules that vary among regions.
- Approach new situations with an open mind and an open heart.
- Be willing to share your expertise on the spot, especially with young people. You may open a window of opportunity for them.

Chapter Eleven

Two Ears, One Mouth

"I only wish I could find an institute that teaches people how to listen. Businesspeople need to listen at least as much as they need to talk. Too many people fail to realize that real communication goes in both directions."

– Lee Iacocca

The one piece of advice that I wish I had been given early in my sales career might surprise you: **A great salesperson must become a good listener.**

There is a reason that the negative stereotype of the salesperson, who never takes a breath and never stops talking, exists. In my first sales job we were taught to walk into a business, introduce yourself and the reason you were there, and start your presentation. We were instructed not to ask permission to show them our presentation. We were taught to just steamroll our way through the entire process. We memorized rebuttals and comebacks to interruptions and objections that people might pose. This model initially seemed perfect for me, because I liked talking to people.

One of my first bosses almost appeared to take it as a personal affront if a potential customer voiced a concern. I cringed at the way he spoke to people. Although he was successful, his caustic personality made me tense. My gut told me that there had to be a better way.

"God gave us two ears and one mouth for a reason, so we ought to listen twice as much as we speak."

– Epictetus

This important axiom was not taught to me. I learned it on the job. I noticed that if I allowed the customer to finish their statement or concern and, even better yet, asked them to clarify why they said that or feel that way, then they would actually tell me how to sell them.

For example, our policy covered all forms of accidents, on the job or off the job, including hobbies and weekend entertainment like water sports and other activities. When potential clients would push back and claim that they had no need, I would ask them what their favorite weekend hobby or entertainment was. After they'd replied, I'd follow up with: "How did you get into that?" Then I would shut up and listen.

After they shared with me their hobbies and interests, I shared some examples of people getting hurt doing exactly the same thing as they did on the weekends. Invariably, they opened up and said, "That almost happened to me." Or "That did happen to my fill-in-the-blank once."

Then I would explain how this plan could come in handy financially if they were ever unfortunate enough to have this happen to them. I was creating in their minds an accident doing something they already participated in, instead of relating the one-size-fits-all examples we were taught to use.

Listen to what your client is telling you instead of thinking about what you are supposed to say next, and they will educate you on how to sell them. By knowing your material and presentation inside and out, you are equipped to do this. You become much more flexible and can react to your customer instead of focusing on your canned spiel.

Have you ever gotten a cold-call and asked a question, and then had the person refuse to go off-script to answer what you asked? Irritating, isn't it? In some industries like ours, the salesperson may have legal reasons that they have to present their product in a certain way.

However, in that situation, you can still acknowledge the question and let the customer know that you will be addressing that concern in just a moment, or will get the answer and get back to them. That reassures your potential client that you genuinely care about their concerns, and aren't simply trying to force something on them.

Being flexible in your thinking and your sales pitch, according to what your potential client has to say, gets back to the topic of the last chapter. You have to be willing to put in the work to learn the products and services your company or organization offers inside and out.

The art of active listening, being present in the moment and not already thinking about what you are going to say next, as well as being flexible enough in your thinking to respond to unexpected objections, questions, or concerns takes practice, practice, and more practice. Especially when you are speaking with someone who was likely a complete stranger just five minutes before.

This may seem really basic, but I've seen it happen all the time. Try to catch yourself when you are tempted to interrupt or talk over a person.

Listening shows respect. Don't assume.

You know what they say about what happens when you assume. Whenever I enter a place of business, I greet the first person I see with this question: 'Are you the owner, or the manager?' I never assume what that person's position is within the company. That question does two things: It establishes that I think that they have some authority, and I save myself from a potentially embarrassing situation by walking in and assuming what someone's position is based on where they happen to be at that moment.

I've taken note of some salespeople who focus all of their attention on one half of a couple, and virtually ignore the other partner. Again, big mistake.

You should direct your comments to both equally, and don't gloss over one partner's questions just because you assume that person doesn't control the money. This is particularly dangerous for male sales reps since, according to studies in our industry, women often control the household finances and make the majority of purchases. A good salesman has to focus his presentation and attention on both sexes.

My wife and I experienced this firsthand when she decided to buy herself a new car. I tagged along. At one car dealership, the moment we stepped out of the car the salesman walked right past my wife and asked me, "What are you looking for today, sir?"

I tried to help him out and said, "I'm not looking for anything. My wife is looking for a new car. You better go ask her."

He was not listening and dove right into his pitch with me. I walked away from him, hoping he'd take the hint and go talk to the potential buyer who was now glaring at him. He still failed to tune in and continued his standard sales pitch to me.

Finally, I held up a hand and said, "Dude, as I tried telling you before, that lovely lady over there getting back in her car is here to buy a new car, a model you have on this lot. You are talking to the wrong person."

At this point my wife was ready to go to the next dealership, and he'd lost the sale. He just stood there with his mouth open and had no idea what had just happened.

The power of observation

In many industries, women sales reps with good observation skills have a huge advantage over a man selling the same product line. I discovered this the moment I became a manager and started field-training both men and women. I subsequently changed the focus of my recruiting efforts as a result.

Let me give you an example. Susan, a middle-aged woman with two years of experience, and I were on an appointment to talk to a lady and her husband about some life insurance on the man. Susan had asked me to ride along. It was Susan's lead, so I was simply observing.

About a third of the way into Susan's presentation the man leaned back in his chair and said, "She doesn't need any life insurance. She can just sell my truck if I die."

Susan completely ignored him and continued talking to the wife about the amount of money she would need when her husband died.

He interrupted again, "Heck, she doesn't need that much money. She will be young enough to get married again."

Susan turned to the man and said, "Sir, you died a few minutes ago and your wife is now trying to figure out how much money she will need to keep her and the kids in this home with food and clothing for the next few years without your paycheck."

He rocked back in his chair and watched. His wife, however, sat up a little straighter, and Susan finalized the sale.

If a salesman had said what Susan said to this man, he may have gotten thrown out of the house. Because Susan knew who the buyer was, she talked woman-to-woman and kept focused on the sale.

Once I realized the influence and buying power women have in most households, I changed the course of my recruiting efforts. More than 65 percent of the people I have hired and trained in the sales industry have been women. Today in the senior health care market, I would say the number of women sales reps in this industry has climbed to well over 80 percent.

> **"To say that a person feels listened to means a lot more than just their ideas get heard. It's a sign of respect. It makes people feel valued."**
>
> **– Deborah Tannen**

Avoid certain topics

When you are in a person's home or place of work, look around. You can tell a lot about what a person cares about by the items they display and their possessions. Are there sports trophies on their shelves? Are they wearing or displaying team logos from a particular high school, college, or pro team? Look at the photos hanging on the wall and what jewelry (such as school rings) they wear. Did you notice any bumper stickers on their vehicle when you came up the driveway?

Now that you have that information, no matter what, stay away from initiating conversations about hot button topics at all costs. Avoid voicing your opinion on politics, religion, or sports teams. If they choose to bring up one of these topics go with the flow, nod, smile, and listen. But if they are adamant about a particular subject, and you choose to debate them, you have signed a death warrant to your sale.

I was training a new agent who had not drunk the Kool-Aid on this rule. On a sales call, a potential client was wearing a shirt with his college logo above the pocket. It just so happened to be the team that this agent's college beat the previous Saturday in a close nail-biter for the rights to go to the playoffs. The agent started bragging about his team beating the man's team. Our potential client's body language told me that sale wasn't happening.

As much as we discussed this pitfall in great detail at our weekly training meetings, you cannot be with each agent on every call. And apparently you cannot anticipate or teach all the topics you should avoid when on a sales call with a client virtually, at home, or at their place of business.

As a manager, I got a call about one of my brand new agents who had told a potential client that he had the ability to heal the man's wife of cancer on the spot and thus qualify her for a health insurance policy with us. "He told me I could answer the question of whether she had cancer as 'no', thanks to his ability," the man told me.

I had a tough time believing what I was hearing and decided I would address this agent at our next weekly meeting. The next day I got another call from a second household, telling me the same thing.

I couldn't believe my ears. I called the agent and insisted he meet me that very day at a coffee shop in his town. When I met with him, I told him about the two complaints I'd gotten. "Is this true?" I asked, still somewhat doubtful.

"Yes, sir. I believe I've been given the gift of healing, and if I can help people I need to do it," he said. He went on to tell me that he felt he had the ability to lay hands on people and heal them of any ailment they might have. I could tell he was serious in his belief and wasn't just using this line to con people into buying a policy they would normally never qualify for.

"Well, you can heal people on your own private time, but you cannot do that on our sales calls," I said. He defended offering his services to these prospective clients, so I had to let him go.

Sleeping on the job

As a manager with one of the companies I worked for, I was required to do ride-alongs with agents every so often to make sure they were following the process and representing our company and the clients in the right manner.

Well, this time around the manager was riding with me to check me out. Bill and I had made several calls that day and made several sales where I had done most of the work, while Bill had mostly just been observing.

When you work in pairs, you decide before you go to the door which salesperson is going to handle the call. The other's job is to just observe. Then after the call the observer grades the presenter and discusses any tweaks that should be made. Now, Bill could not keep quiet anywhere he went and kept interrupting the flow of my presentations.

Finally, I'd had enough of his interruptions, and back in the car I told him, "Look, I just want you to see what I can do. On this next call, please be quiet and do not talk at all."

We arrived at this house about 6:00 pm, right at dusk. I started the presentation, and Bill started interrupting. I stopped and glared at him. He then looked at the client and said, "Doug here is one of our best agents we have and will take good care of you. Do you mind if I take your newspaper over to the couch and read it while you two talk?"

She looked a little surprised, but I nodded yes to her and she said, "Sure." I then continued with my presentation.

About 15 minutes later, we heard the most awful noise coming from the living room. Bill was sound asleep, with his head tilted back, snoring up a storm. We both had a giggle about it. I told her he had driven most of the day prior getting down here to eastern Montana, and we had worked till late last night, and he was just really tired. I continued with my presentation.

I was working on filling out her application, and she asked if I wanted some cookies and a cup of coffee. "Sure," I said.

"What about Bill?" she asked.

"I'll go check." I went into the living room, and Bill still had his head back and was still snoring up a storm. I picked up the newspaper and placed it over his head. He just kept snoring away.

Back in the kitchen, I enjoyed some great cookies and finalized our business. Upon getting up to leave I made a loud noise, and Bill woke right up, grabbed both sides of the paper across his face and acted like he was reading it and had never been sleeping at all. The client and I looked at each other and had a good laugh. I started telling her goodbye and thanked her for her time.

We headed back toward the motel and restaurant. I started giving him a hard time about going to sleep, and he denied ever having been asleep. I told him we heard his snoring clear over at the table. Bill continued to deny he had gone to sleep. He insisted he was reading the newspaper and heard every word of our conversation.

Bill was hard-headed and would never admit that he was wrong about anything. It was killing him not knowing how the appointment went, and if I made the sale or not, but he was not going to ask me that directly.

I decided to have some fun, and so did not volunteer any information. So Bill started doing the manager review that we do after every joint call. He was supposed to be grading me and making comments about my presentation that he observed.

Well, he did not see a thing, and here he was trying to review my performance. Since he could not comment on something he had not seen, he started asking me leading questions like, "Well, how did you think you did on the close?" He was digging to see if I sold something. My reply, "It was okay, but I could have done better."

He countered with, "Why do you think she made the decision she did?"

My comeback: "I have no idea right now."

He countered, "Could it have been something you two had discussed?"

I replied: "It could have."

This back-and-forth went on all night during dinner. Bill never once asked me directly if I made the sale or not. He refused to admit he fell sleep. And I never volunteered that information.

I could not outright laugh at him and let him know I knew the truth, but inside I was rolling with laughter all the next day as we continued to work. He kept working me, and I continued to play dumb.

Knock-Knock Moments

- Develop your listening skills and use them lavishly.
- Never ignore someone and assume that they aren't the decision maker.
- Be respectful of everyone.
- Never be so busy talking all the time that you miss key information—verbal or non-verbal.

Chapter Twelve

When Life Throws You a Curve, Lean Into It

"Our greatest weakness lies in giving up. The most certain way to succeed is always to try just one more time."

– Thomas A. Edison

Sustainable success can only come as a result of a win-win for you and your client. It's the culmination of your 1) **effort**, 2) **attitude**, 3) **communication skills**, and 4) **product knowledge** that will produce the results you're seeking.

What you have to be ready to apply in each of those four areas is creative thinking. In sales, you have to be prepared all the time for the unexpected. If you expect that you are going to run into new—sometimes downright crazy—situations, questions, objections, and unique individuals on a daily basis, then you won't be caught off guard.

It pays to be nimble and quick in your thinking.

In the dead of winter in eastern Montana, I was training a new agent. We were having one of the worst winters in years, with an extraordinary amount of snow accumulation.

The local ranchers depend upon either their stored stocks of hay cut the year before or on the snow melting, off and on, during the winter, allowing their stock to eat green grass. This winter was so bad and lasted so long that many of the ranchers were running out of hay and were having to buy it from one of the Southern states.

We had been trying to get an appointment with this rancher for a while, with no results. We made one last attempt to see him. When we called, he said he was expecting a semi-truck load of hay late that afternoon. "If you want to come on out this morning, I'll make time to see you," he said.

So away we went, driving 60+ miles one way on snow-covered gravel roads to reach his place. About halfway there, we came up behind a semi-truck loaded down with hay with Texas plates. There were no cell phones in those days, so we looked at each other.

"This has to be some other rancher's hay, because he is about six hours ahead of schedule for our rancher," I said.

We had worked weeks on getting this appointment and needed to keep it, so we kept on driving. It was impossible to get around the truck on this narrow road with four-foot-deep snow drifts on each side.

We could see the turn-off to the rancher's place ahead. We were already running an hour late due to being caught behind the semi driving only 25 mph across the county. Then our hearts dropped as we saw the truck pulling into the same ranch where we were headed. What were the odds that this was his truckload of hay?

We saw the rancher instructing the truck driver as to which barn to back his semi-truck up to, and then he walked over to us.

We made our introductions, and were apologizing for being late due to following the truck, when he held his hand up and said, "Sorry, fellas. It's going to take the driver and me at least four hours to unload those square bales. You'll have to come back at another time."

We were prepared for an insurance presentation in a nice, warm house at a kitchen table, and were both in suits, ties, and dress shoes.

I said, "We would love to help you unload your hay if you have some overalls and extra boots."

He declined initially, but I told him that we had already marked off the morning to talk to him and his family. "We don't have anything else to do, so why not let us stay and help?"

The agent I was training looked at me like I was crazy, but I gave him a signal that all would be all right. The rancher saw that I was serious. "Come on, boys; I'll show you were you can get changed," he said, turned to me one more time on the way to the house, and asked, "Are you sure?"

This time both of us answered, "You bet."

Long story short, we helped them unload the entire load of hay in just under two hours. But I took advantage of every minute of that time. After going through some small talk to get to know each other, and asking him a ton of questions about his ranch operation, I dove in and started talking to him about our company and the insurance plans we had as we were carrying bales of hay back and forth from the truck to the barn.

"You will get all you want in life, if you help enough other people get what they want."

– Zig Ziglar

Once we finished unloading, he invited us to the house for some coffee and to warm up. On the way to the house, he was shaking our hands and thanking us over and over again for the help. As we walked into the house and started talking our boots off, he introduced us to his wife and informed her that these two guys were going to explain to her what I had explained to him in the barn and asked her, "Sweetheart, can you make some coffee and bring the ranch checkbook to the kitchen table?"

BANG! The ultimate buying signal.

Mind your manners at all costs

Early in my career in eastern Montana, I had an appointment way out in the country at a farm with a woman who had recently lost her husband

and needed some health insurance. Upon arriving I found out that her two sons and their families had moved back home to help mom take care of this huge farm. "I need health insurance and life insurance on me, the boys, and their families," she announced.

I was licking my chops at the thought of this huge multiple sale. After two hours of showing her the options available to them and then filling out multiple applications, she brought out a huge piece of pie and a cup of coffee.

The coffee was great, but the pie was sour cream raisin pie. Did you hear me? A sour cream raisin pie. I hated every bite but forced myself to choke it down, and faked my delight as best I could while eating it.

You never want to insult a client by refusing their hospitality, and I wasn't about to break that rule.

Upon arriving home I explained to my wife the great day of production that I had, but I also told her about the terrible sour cream raisin pie this lady served me that I had to choke down, all while smiling and moaning in delight.

She had heard similar stories, as clients were always serving me all sorts of homemade cookies, brownies, cakes, and pies on my visits with them. Some good, some bad.

A month went by, and all of the policies came back. I called her to set an appointment to deliver them. "I need a few minutes with each of the adults to go over the coverages you purchased for them, and they each need to sign for the policies," I said.

We set up the appointment, and she said, "I'll cook a fried chicken dinner for us all."

I arrived on time. We got the paperwork out and got it completed, and then she served a fantastic fried chicken dinner with mashed potatoes and other goodies. Then she asked everyone if they wanted a piece of pie, and they all said they did.

Remembering the last piece of pie she served me, I said, "I am too full and cannot handle a piece." I was worried that the only pie she could make was that blasted sour cream raisin pie.

She then served fresh pieces of apple and pumpkin pies to the others, which got my attention. "You know, I think I will have a piece after all," I said.

She emerged from the kitchen with a huge piece of sour cream raisin pie. "I talked to your office gal and she told me this was your favorite pie, and that you have been talking about it non-stop," she said. "I also made a whole one for you to take back with you, and I wrote out the recipe for her."

At this point, I realized that my wife Shirley, aka "my office gal", had pranked me good.

"You don't pay the price for success—you enjoy the benefits of success."

– Zig Ziglar

Never give up

When selling accident/disability plans, we cold-called on businesses door-to-door and asked to speak to the owner/manager. We showed them our product and, regardless if they bought or not, we would ask permission to talk to all of their employees. We typically would then set up in the breakroom.

At a bank in east Texas, I had received permission to talk to all of the employees as they would take a break. When leaving that town to drive home, I drove through the drive-in window to cash a check and realized I had not spoken to the teller now helping me at the window. She had purposely avoided the break room, so she "would not be sold".

It was almost closing time, so I pulled out a brochure, pressed it up to the window in the drive-thru, and started my presentation. This only took three minutes and I closed. She was so impressed with my persistence and the coverage we were offering that she bought the policy right there in the drive-thru window, and this sale proved to me that you should never give up no matter how fast they run or how well they hide. Bonus: Always make one more call before you call it a day.

Show me the money

You haven't really made a sale until you collect payment, and sometimes getting the money requires creativity, too. I had written multiple plans on the owner and employees of a large real estate office, and the owner was going to pay for them all. It took me all week to catch everyone and get the applications completed.

On Friday I stopped by his office to pick up the check, and his secretary said what every salesperson hates to hear, "He's left for the day early and forgot to sign the check."

"Do you happen to know where he went?" I asked.

"He has a tee time at the local golf course for 3 o'clock this afternoon," she said.

Well, this was a huge sale for me. I had worked all week on it and wanted to be paid Monday when I turned the business in, so I asked for the check and explained that I wanted to try and catch him before he started his game, "because you and everyone else will not be covered next week as we had discussed." She agreed and away I went.

By the time I got there, his group had already teed off and were starting their round. I knew they were going to be out on the course for at least three more hours. But I had played this course before and I also knew that there was a paved road that bordered the fairway and tee box on the third hole. Being a little impatient, considering the two-hour drive home and really wanting to get paid, I drove around to the third hole, parked my car, walked through a ditch, and climbed over the fence in my suit and tie and waited for them to come up to the third tee box.

When his foursome walked up, he started laughing his butt off. Being a real estate agent, he knew why I was there. I got that business, and the other three businessmen in his golfing party were so impressed by my persistence and follow-through that they became clients of mine in the following weeks.

Sometimes it takes magic to close a sale

I was training an agent and it was his turn to handle the entire sales process, including the close and writing up the application. My job was to support him but mainly just to observe. Well, this young couple had an 18-month-old girl who kept crawling up in a chair at the kitchen table, so she could see what was going on. She was attracted to all this colorful paper and brochures, and kept crawling across the table and disrupting the presentation. Neither parent did a thing.

The chair she was using was next to me, so I repeatedly picked her up and placed her back on the floor as the three continued to talk.

Well, I used to do magic for kids' birthday parties, and so I reached into my pocket and grabbed a quarter. I showed it to the little girl and made it disappear. That slowed her down, so I did it again. She lost interest quickly and started for the chair again. I made the quarter disappear and then magically pulled it out of her ear. Well, this stopped her in her tracks, but she did not fully understand what just happened. There was a huge grey cat lying on the counter right behind her head, so I made the quarter disappear and then magically pulled it out of the cat's ear.

This just amazed her. She grabbed that cat and sat down on the floor. I was relieved to have distracted her from the table. A good ten minutes went by, when all of a sudden, this cat shrieked. When I looked down on the floor next to me this little girl had a headlock on this cat and two fingers shoved into its ear, trying to find another quarter.

I quickly reached down and swatted her hand loose from around the cat. The poor creature screamed one more time and took off. The parents looked over and asked what was wrong.

"Sorry, I must have accidently stepped on your cat's tail," I said. Everybody went back to business. I took a really big breath and then sat on my hands. Never again did I use my magic on a sales call.

Making something seem scarce can make it more desirable

As a veteran agent, I was driving back through Forsyth, Montana, one Friday night after being on the road all week long. The highway was blocked due to a train derailment. I pulled up to a bar that served great sandwiches to get something to eat and to wait out the road closure. The place was packed with travelers and railroad workers, who all had the same idea.

I grabbed the only stool available at the bar. The guy sitting next to me worked on the railroad and was in the process of tying a good drunk on. I was in a suit and tie, and he started bugging me about what I did for a living. I told him at first that I was in sales. But he insisted on knowing what kind of sales. So I finally told him I was a life insurance agent.

Right away he held his hands up and said, "I don't need any more damn life insurance, so don't even start on me."

I didn't want to hear his bull all night either, so I decided to have a little fun. "That's good to hear, because I am all sold out of life insurance tonight," I said, just as the waitress plopped my sandwich and fries down on the counter.

There was a very long pause in the conversation, but he couldn't help himself. He said, "Bull, you can't be out of life insurance. There is no limit on the amount of life insurance available. Someone can have as much as they want. Correct?"

"That's kinda true," I said. "There may be no limit on how much you could have, but I am sold out this week. I do not have any more life insurance left." I just wanted him to shut up and let me eat my meal. I was done working this week.

After another long pause, he once again said, "Bull, you can't be out of life insurance. Are you telling me you could not write me up another $100,000 policy right now?"

I said, "Nope, I am all out."

"I am 35 years old. What would a $100,000 policy cost on me if you weren't sold out?" he demanded to know.

I pulled my rate book out of my suit coat pocket and quoted him a price. You would have thought he had won the lottery. "See, I told you. I knew you were not sold out," he said.

I put the rate book up and said, "Sir, that's just the price you would pay if I had any available, but I am all sold out and couldn't sell it to you if I wanted to."

"Doug, I want some life insurance and I am willing to pay the annual price you just quoted me," he said, and then reached into his pocket and pulled out a checkbook and slapped it down on the bar between us.

I looked over at him and repeated, "Sorry, I'm all out."

He opened the checkbook, looked at the business card I had given him earlier, wrote out a check to my company for the annual premium, and slapped it down and said, "There is my payment. Now go get an application and write me up."

This man had just called my bluff. Thinking fast and with a large lump in my throat, I said, "I had written the last application I had with me earlier today and cannot sign you up, because I don't have any more applications. I am sold out."

He said, "You go out to your car and check again, young man."

I went out to my car, opened the trunk and took out a new application, crumpled it up and placed it on the pavement and stepped on it a couple of times. Well, the app was still in good enough shape to use but looked pretty beat up.

I went back in holding it up, and said, "I found one last app in the bottom of the trunk, but I don't know if we can use it."

He placed it on the bar and started trying to rub out all the wrinkles and said, "I think we can make this work, Doug."

I then wrote up a nice life insurance sale with this railroader's help.

Mike kept that policy for years and even though I never saw him again, I bet he had a little smile on his face every time he paid the annual premium, knowing he proved to that young salesman you can never be sold out of life insurance.

Knock-Knock Moments

- Going the extra mile can payoff big.
- Accept whatever hospitable act comes your way.
- Take advantage of the unexpected opportunities that fall into your lap.
- Sometimes it may take a little magic to close the deal.
- Leave 'em wanting more.

Chapter Thirteen

Seal the Deal

"Amazing things will happen when you listen to the customer."

– Jonathan Midenhall

Before we chat about the steps to closing a sale, do you know what the #1 deal killer is? **A bad first impression**. Remember the six-second rule. That's the amount of time it takes a potential client to size you up. You never get another chance to make another first impression with that prospect.

A quick review: Know your product inside and out and be prepared. Dress for your audience. Avoid hot button topics. Be on time. Don't assume who the decision-maker is.

On some occasions, you run into issues that right off the bat are unavoidable and unsalvageable. In those instances, after just a moment, I am looking for the rip cord on my parachute and some way to get out of there quickly yet gracefully.

Once I was on a ride-along with an agent, and we had an appointment to see a rancher and his wife that this agent knew very well. We arrived on time, and the rancher invited us in and said the wife would be joining us in a moment. The rancher was washing dinner dishes and the agent stood by, helping him dry those dishes.

I took a seat at the kitchen table which faced a hallway, when the wife emerged from the shower unaware that we were there. She came up the hallway with her head down, drying her hair with a towel, which is all she had. I cleared my throat to try to alert her, we locked eyes, and she screamed and bolted for the master bedroom, which was at the end of the hallway.

The rancher turned to me and asked, "Was she coming down the hall naked?"

I nodded, and he excused himself and headed back to talk to her. After a few minutes, he came back into the kitchen, shrugged his shoulders and said, "Sorry, fellas. I don't believe we'll be discussing a policy tonight." There was nothing left to do but to excuse ourselves politely and go to the next call.

Tap in to your intuition

How can you use your intuition better in making sales, and how can you learn to be better at tapping in to your senses? Through experience and observation. In a classroom or by watching a training video online, for example, you can teach some of the signs of interest and the body language that communicates buying signals. But your intuition will only get better in watching for and reading these signs with experience and observing people in different situations.

There is no other way to get good experience than just doing it yourself over and over. Ideally, you will create many situations that you will handle correctly, but your drive to gather experience will also create some that go badly or that you wish you'd never gotten yourself into in the first place. But the best way to look at a bad call is to think of it as a learning experience and try to find a golden nugget that could help you in the future.

Often, I have walked into a home or place of business that gave out a great vibe, and I knew this was going to be a good appointment.

Other times, after just a few minutes, I had a gut feeling this appointment was not going to turn out well. With experience, my hunches got better and usually turned out to be correct.

Your intuition will be fed by your observational skills. What are you seeing, what are you hearing, and what are you feeling? Pay attention, and you will activate intuition.

For example, you need to quickly sort out a prospect's communication and personality style. How do you do that? By testing them. Here's an example:

When entering their home or business tell them you have some literature to lay out for them to review and ask them if you could all sit at the dining table or, if at an office, at the conference table. If they agree to allow you to set up the room and the seating arrangements, they are in a lower dominance position and prone to suggestions.

If they insist on staying where they are, or offer an alternative place or arrangement, then they are demonstrating a higher dominance and tend to like to take command and control the situation. I can deal with either one, but now I know what type of client I am dealing with and what frame of mind they are in. That means I can adjust my presentation and approach accordingly.

Open-ended questions help close the sale

The smartest salespeople get prospects to open up by asking a series of open-ended questions. When you ask the right questions in the right way, you can end up getting your prospects to do all the selling for you. If you listen, you'll learn a lot about what the prospect wants from your product or service, which means you can laser-focus your presentation on just those points that will sell most effectively.

Here are three things the right questions can give you:

1. Thoughtful, open-ended questions help you confirm whether or not the prospect is a good fit for what you are selling. **Open-ended questions** are broad and need to be answered in detail. While **closed-ended questions** are narrow in focus and are usually answered with a single word like yes and no.

2. These open-ended questions help you to identify the prospect's hot button, which allows you to fine-tune your pitch and recommendations.

3. By getting prospects to talk about various aspects of your products'/services' benefits and what they think about those benefits, you sneak the information past the prospect's salesperson filter.

Here are some examples of open-ended questions I've found effective:

- What experiences, good or bad, have you had with this type of product or service (or with this company)?
- How long have you been with your existing company?
- What do you like best about them?
- What are they not providing you that you feel is important?
- What qualities or benefits are most important to you when considering this purchase?
- What would you like this product/service to do for you?

If the prospect only provides a brief answer, then ask a clarifying question such as:

- You probably have a very good reason for saying that. Would you tell me why?
- Can you tell me more about that?
- That's very interesting. Can you be more specific?

Carefully considered questions during the presentation that are designed to elicit information can be one of the most important tools at your disposal to help you close the sale. These questions can provoke your prospect to name chief concerns/objections or ask specific questions about whatever you are selling. When you get them to that point, solving those concerns and any objections, you usually get a buying signal.

Keeping the Deal Sealed

People can tell when your main goal is to make a sale, and you don't really care about them. They just sense it.

In sales, sometimes you'll come across a client who buys from you but then suffers from buyers' remorse and will test your patience. They are filled with doubts. They wonder if they could have gotten a better deal. If they made the right choice. You may come to regret ever having sold to that customer.

Not so fast. Remember how I said there are no bad prospects? Let me tell you why these never-satisfied worry-warts may turn into one of your favorite customers if you just take the time to figure out what their main concern is. It may not be your product or service at all.

Medicare Supplements, which are supplemental health plans for seniors on Medicare, vary in benefits and costs. I had helped a lady sign up for a new health plan after she had sent in a card to my company, requesting information.

Betty had recently lost her husband, along with the group health plan that his employment had provided. She had never had to make one of these types of decisions by herself until that day I visited her in Ekalaka, Montana, which is located in the far southeast corner of the state. She took my recommendation of what type of coverage she needed and bought a new policy.

Like clockwork, once a month I would get a phone call from Betty, complaining about the supplemental plan that she had purchased from me. "Doug, would you please drop by and explain to me why my plan is so much different than my friend's coverage?" she'd ask. Or the next time she would call and ask why her plan costs $16 a month more than the plans of the other ladies at the senior citizen center.

Each call would end with a plea for me to drop by and explain away whatever was troubling her that week.

It was those words DROP BY that got my goat. Drop by! Drop by? Betty lived a five-hour roundtrip from where I lived. Ekalaka was not officially in the middle of nowhere, but you can see it from there. This elderly widow was asking me to "just drop by".

I would try to pacify her concerns by phone, but the moment she would talk to someone else at the center who had some other coverage, or she read a flyer sent to her by another company, she would get upset and confused and call me again.

I did make routine trips down towards Ekalaka every quarter to visit clients and try to pick up some new customers. On one of my next trips to this area, I stopped by Betty's house to visit and help calm her down and reassure about her previous health care decision.

Upon my arrival she pulled out a ton of junk mail that insurance competitors had sent her. She had been trying unsuccessfully to compare them with what she had and was only getting more confused and frustrated. I went out to the car and got a box out of my trunk and brought it into her house and asked her if she could help me help her.

"Betty, what I'd like you to do is take all of the junk mail you receive each week and put it all in this box," I said. "Once a quarter I will stop by, and I will go over each one of them with you. I will explain how and why they differ from what you already have."

I emphasized that she should not be opening this mail until I arrived on my next trip. This project would help keep her from worrying about her coverage until I could sit down and go over all of it with her face-to-face. "But you will also be helping me, as it lets me know what products other companies and agents are marketing in this area so I can be prepared to compare them with other customers who have the same questions you may have," I said.

Asking for her help allowed me to transform a difficult client into an ally. Plus, this project helped calm her down and gave her something to do in her retirement years.

Upon my next visit to Betty three months later, I was greeted by a newly positive and happy Betty. She was dressed up, had cookies and coffee ready, and was humming a tune as she went about setting the table.

She brought the box of junk mail out (all unopened), and as I had promised, we took time to open each and go through them all. Then I asked her if I could use her phone and phonebook to call some local leads that I had brought with me.

"I could help with that, Doug," she offered. To my delight, she knew almost everyone I was looking up and even knew the phone number for most. On a couple of them she even told me they were out of town and when they would be back, saving me the effort of calling.

On the next trip to Ekalaka, as I knocked on Betty's door, she yelled, "Come on in!" As I walked into the house, I could hear her on the phone saying, "I have to go. My boss just walked in." This time not only did Betty have the cookies and coffee ready, but she had a list of people who wanted to talk to me about insurance when I got to town on this trip.

The box of junk mail was sitting on the floor, and I asked her, "Should we go through all of that first?"

"No, I don't want to see any of that junk," she said. "You just take it with you."

And we started working on setting up some appointments.

This exchange happened quarterly. Betty's entire personality changed, as she now had a purpose, and I had found a fantastic new friend and ally. All because I practiced patience and empathy, and continued to listen long after the original deal was sealed.

I miss you, Betty.

Knock-Knock Moments

- You won't get that homerun if you never take a turn at bat.
- Learn to listen to your gut when making a sales call.
- Practice the art of asking great questions and letting the prospect tell you how to sell them.
- Kindness can transform the most difficult customer into an ally.
- When customers have a complaint, listen. Let them vent. Most of the time they fix it themselves.

Chapter Fourteen

Brand You

"It's important to build a personal brand because it's the only thing you're going to have. Your reputation online and in the new business world is pretty much the game, so you've got to be a good person. You can't hide anything and, more importantly, you've got to be out there at some level."

– Gary Vaynerchuck

When you are in sales, you may not think of yourself as a personal brand. That's a mistake. But I didn't think like that either early on in my career. Because I cut my hair, shaved my beard, changed the way I dressed and stopped wearing my earring, I thought of myself as a company man. Inside I was still a rebel at heart, but with the clientele I was calling on I felt like I couldn't outwardly display that side of me.

With experience, I came to understand that I wasn't just representing a company. With each encounter, sales call, presentation and follow up, as well as in my everyday life in our community, I was building a personal brand. And although how you present yourself is part of that brand, the bigger part of your personal brand goes deeper.

These are just few questions that will help you think about what your personal brand is:

- Do you come across as someone who genuinely cares about your customers?
- Are you honest in your business dealings?
- Do you deliver a quality product/service and work to make it right if something goes wrong?
- Can your customers count on you to be reliable, consistent, and competent?
- Are you authentic? Empathetic? Kind?
- What drives you to do what you do?

Ask a few close friends and family members to name the top five qualities you possess that come to mind when they think of you. Now ask the same question of a work colleague, a long-time customer, and a new customer. If you get widely divergent answers, you likely aren't being authentic in your work life. Do some soul searching to figure out how to get the two to align.

> **"Your personal brand is a promise to your clients… a promise of quality, consistency, competency, and reliability."**
>
> **– Jason Hartman**

People like to buy from people they know and trust. They hate to be "sold". Does that always apply? Pretty much in every sales situation. People do not buy from someone they do not like or do not want to be around, no matter how good the product or service. The retail sales environment where the buyer has little or at least less choice or control over who they are buying from is about the only place where customers may still buy despite a negative experience. However, with so many brick-and-mortar stores closing—from department stores to strip mall anchors—consumers are signaling more and more that they won't put up with poor attitudes and poor service.

> **"Your brand is a gateway to your true work. You know you are here to do something—to create something or help others in some way. The question is, how can you set up your life and work so that you can do it? The answer lies in your brand. When you create a compelling brand, you attract people who want the promise of your brand— which you deliver."**
>
> **– Dave Buck**

I always tell agents: **Tell the truth**. If for no other reason, the truth is a lot easier to remember later. Most potential clients sense it when you are trying to get the sale at all costs. If you don't know something say you don't know but will get back to the prospect with the answer.

Sure, there are salespeople who do well for themselves by shading the truth, think nothing of breaking their promises, lie when it benefits them, and don't think twice about any of these negative acts. But in almost every instance when I've known someone like that the chickens come home to roost, and an unscrupulous salesperson does not survive in this line of work for the long haul.

The internet has made it a lot harder to hide who you are. A simple Google search and quick peek at social media profiles turns up information on most anyone you care to look up.

When I decided to give insurance sales a second try, I joined an office that had several veteran agents who had been selling these products for years. I quickly deduced that some knew tricks and shortcuts that the managers would not dare bring up in a meeting or teach us. So I watched and listened to these veterans closely to see what I could pick up.

Some veterans such Larry, Paul, and Jack had successful careers, knew a fair amount of shortcuts, did everything compliantly and by the book, but their production was not at the level that I wanted mine to be at. Now Bud, Hank, and Ted outwrote everyone in the office each month, but I quickly picked up that they weren't playing it by the book and were burning a few bridges along the way.

The first sign that tipped me off to how the latter three might be bridge burners was that when phone calls would come into the office for them, they would ask who was on the line before they would agree to talk to them. When they heard some names, they quickly raised a hand and said, "I've gotta go." And they would leave the office.

I discovered that they were giving clients misleading information or were using distasteful sales tactics in order to make sales. They subsequently dodged calls from these customers. Their success came from the churn-and-burn marketing approach that I thought I'd left behind.

How did I know? In more than one case, I was faced with cleaning up the fallout from their sales tactics. I had a lead come in on a person way out in the boonies back up against a mountain range in central Montana. I drove for hours to get to this house. The last five miles was on a one-lane gravel road.

Upon my arrival, the homeowner was standing in the doorway and asked me who I was and to quickly state my business. I told him my name and what company I worked for and the reason for my visit. "Just a minute," he said, and stepped back into the house.

When he returned he had a shotgun in hand, put the barrel under my chin, and said, "I swore the next person that ever came to my front door from your company would never leave my property alive and would be buried in the ditch over there where I dump my trash."

I tried to stay calm and said, "I can see you are upset, but before you do so could you please explain what happened so maybe I can help correct the issue?"

I had a gut feeling what had happened, because the week prior I had stumbled upon another lady not too far from this location to whom Hank had misrepresented the coverage he was selling, took the check, and never would return her calls. I had made a phone call to the home office and got her a full refund on her purchase.

This homeowner lowered the gun down from my chin, but kept it pointed in my direction while he related a similar experience with Hank. I assured him I could fix it and asked to use his phone. He agreed, and I called the home office and explained what had happened. The company not only gave him a full refund on the money he paid, but offered him the policy he originally wanted and paid the premium for a year. He finally calmed down, put the gun down, and apologized for his behavior.

Even though I never went back out to his house, I did return his calls. These two cases among others were turned over to the company's legal department, and Hank was history.

Everybody serves as an example – a good one or a bad one

There are a lot of personalities in sales, and you certainly do not have to mirror mine to build a successful brand in sales. But early on, I was exposed to some personalities that I knew either had no long-range hope of building a lasting career or that I just had no interest in mirroring.

One such person was a manager I had who flashed his success in everyone's face by the way he dressed, the flashy jewelry he wore, and the late model Cadillacs he drove, but mainly by the way he talked to people. He was never wrong about any subject and would push his way into any door even at the risk of getting the police called on him.

He never listened to a client. He was going to talk and no one else could get a word in edgewise. He taught me zero relationship-building skills. But yet he made a ton of sales. Thinking back on it, sometimes I think people bought just to get him to leave. I determined while working with him that his was not a model of success I wanted to follow.

Identify your strengths

What do you want to be known for? If you are in sales, you must answer that question. Whether you know it or not, you bring your personal brand to each selling opportunity.

Eventually I realized that I wanted to be known as a knowledgeable, empathetic salesperson who really listened to my clients' needs and who made the entire process smooth and enjoyable for all.

Because I've always been a happy, fun-loving person who enjoys a good laugh, before long I found myself wanting to inject some humor into my conversations with clients and prospects. People often tell me I'm funny, but I'm more of the reactive and improvisational humorist. Quick with a bit of wit, but based on the situation at hand. I have trouble when asked to be funny on demand.

Now, trust me, I have thousands of jokes and stories in my repertoire. But my memory is terrible, so my humor comes out situationally and sometimes unintentionally.

With humor you have to be careful about how, when, or if you should use it at all. Especially when selling.

Within just a few months of starting my career in sales, I was promoted to a district manager position in Texas. Within a week of that promotion, all the salespeople in the state and their spouses were invited to a convention in Dallas. I was looking forward to finally meeting the other top salespeople I had been competing with each week. Then I got a phone call from my boss, telling me that I would be joining four other Texas managers in rolling out a brand-new product to all attendees during this meeting, and he would be sending me my portion of the speech.

You're kidding me. ON STAGE. Remember, I was the last guy in my class in school who ever wanted to get in front of the class and do anything. Now I was going to have to get on stage in front of thousands of people and give a SPEECH.

I studied my part and was the fourth manager in this presentation. I stood up straight and gave it my all. I had no idea how I did or what I said. Walking off stage everyone in the wings was telling me I did great, but it scared the daylights out of me so badly that I could not remember what I had just said to these folks. As I was standing there in the wings still in a daze, the last manager to present on this new plan was now going to show everyone how to properly complete the new application that came with it.

Just before he went on stage, he turned to me in a panic and said, "Doug, the person who was going to be my prospect completing this application backed out. Can you help me out and fill in?"

Now, how hard can playing the prospect part be? So I said, "Sure, let's go do it."

As he started down the application, he asked me my name. I handled that perfectly. But that was the last thing I handled well. On stage, I must have still been in a daze from my presentation and was not thinking clearly.

He asked me my address. We had just moved, and I could not remember the new address, but instead of making something up I sat there like a stone trying to remember my new address as laughter started to rise in the room. I flushed red, and he finally said, "Can you ask your wife?"

I stood and looked across the room, but with the stage lights in my eyes I could not find her, so I just yelled, "Shirley?"

She shouted out our address, and he wrote it down. He then asked me my date of birth. Once again, I froze. Again, I stood up and yelled "Shirley!"

To which she responded with my date of birth. Everyone in the place was now roaring with laughter. "Now," he said, "I assume your wife's name is Shirley."

I nodded yes. Then he asked me, "What is Shirley's date of birth?"

I could not remember that either and slowly stood up. The entire crowd beat me to it and yelled out in unison, "SHIRLEY!"

She gave her date of birth. This brought the house down.

Now he had to ask some medical questions and asked me if I ever had any surgeries. I said, "I had a knee operation a few years ago."

He asked me the date. Well, I did not even have to stand this time, the entire crowd yelled out, "SHIRLEY!" and roared with laughter.

We finished the presentation and walked towards the wings with a standing ovation going on. The CEO and the President of the company, who I had never meet before, were waiting to go on with their speeches. They stopped the two of us, shook our hands, and said, "Great routine, guys. Your practice really paid off."

I said, "Yes, sir, it always does."

At times with a client, I've overplayed my funny guy self and could tell I'd stepped over an invisible boundary, offended, or put off someone. You have to be able to read your audience, and definitely stay away from any hot button topics like religion, politics, or sex.

Know when it's time to reinvent yourself

Change is a constant in every industry I can think of. Sales basics may remain the same, but almost everything else about sales shifts: distribution, marketing tactics, technology, or the best way to reach your audience. You name it, and it's going to be different soon. So how do you know when you need a brand check-up?

Make sure your brand always fits your mission and values. But keep in mind that your brand is never static. It is a living, breathing asset that should change and evolve as you and your market change. Products come and go. Regulations change, and customers' needs change. So you need to keep growing your expertise, and the skills and services that you offer, or you quickly become outdated and forgotten in your industry and in the marketplace.

Continually ask your clientele for feedback. This will help gauge what tweaks or changes you need to be making to your brand or messaging. I send out emails or newsletters to my clients in order to keep my brand and expertise front and center in their minds. At the bottom of one of these messages to my clients I will attach a hotlink to my website, Facebook, or new advertising piece, along with a request: "I would really appreciate you taking a look at my new website and give me your opinion. Oh, by the way, would you mind sending this email on to a friend or relative? I would really like their opinion as well." Some people may not respond to an email selling them something, but everyone likes to provide their opinion. I get great feedback and have picked up many new clients who received that forwarded email.

Be careful about jumping onboard too quickly to the hottest new trend, product, or marketing approach. If it communicates the wrong message to your target market, or ends up being noncompliant, you may cause damage to your brand that will be hard to undo. If it is a good direction to go, let others work the bugs out. There will be plenty of clients still available for you to jump on board the band-wagon a little later.

That means you'd better be willing to give yourself a brand check-up on a regular basis. Is your behavior in line with your stated values?

Do you treat your customers the way you'd want to be treated?

Do you wake up each day, proud of the career path you've chosen?

I recently went to see Sinbad (David Adkins), a 6'4" comedian who had become famous in the late 1990s. That night he told us how he had to change his brand midway into his career, at the risk of losing his fan base, and what prompted him to do so.

Sinbad has made quite a few movies, but he got his start doing standup comedy and, like many comedians in that time period, had started using cuss words and foul language in his performance as was the cool thing to do. Sinbad was raised in Michigan, and his father was a preacher.

One night his grandmother attended one of his stand-up perfor-mances, and Sinbad was anxious to get her reaction. Even though he had brought the house down that night, his grandmother looked him in the eye and said, "I'm ashamed of you, David. You were never brought up using that type of language, and you were funny then. What makes you feel talking that trash makes you funny now?" And she walked away.

Sinbad had a deep heart-to-heart with himself and said, "Grandma was 100% right." He changed his routine, and from that night on quit using foul language in his performance and went on to be very successful.

Knock-Knock Moments

- Determine what you want your brand to be.
- Use humor wisely.
- Give yourself a brand check-up.
- Be true to your values.

Chapter Fifteen

The Big Payoff of Investing in Relationships

*"Personal relationships are the fertile soil from which
all advancement, all success, all achievement in
real life grows."*

– Ben Stein

How do you make sure that a customer becomes a repeat customer and ideally stays that all-important customer for life? By building a genuine relationship and earning their respect.

The most important thing a buyer wants from a seller is to know that you genuinely care about their needs more than you care about making a sale. They do not care how much you know until they know how much you care.

I start working on building a relationship right out of the chute. Relationship-building starts from the moment you introduce yourself, during the warm-up, throughout the sales process, and then continues once they become clients.

With the kind of sales career this book is designed to help you build, sustainable success can only come as a result of a win-win for you and your client. Genuine sales—where you are making your best effort to meet your clients' needs and keep yourself and them informed about changes and improvements in the services or products and/or special deals or better prices that arise—will produce the results you're seeking.

A satisfied client will often give referrals before you even ask

How do you know if you've been successful in your quest to start building a relationship? Here's your sign: When at the end of that sale, you ask for a referral and they readily recommend their friends and relatives, you know you have secured a client for life. A satisfied customer will share the news of finding you and the products or services you offer as quickly as they will share with their friends and family a great new dining experience they have discovered.

Sometimes you may get off on the wrong foot or encounter an awkward situation. Don't despair. If you maintain calm and keep the end goal in mind the relationship may be salvageable because, again, people sense when you genuinely care.

I stopped by a house for which I had a lead card that faced the highway and knocked on the door. No one answered, so I knocked a little harder. A German shepherd came flying around the corner of the house and let me know who was in charge, and it wasn't me. At the speed he was coming at me, I knew I looked like fresh meat to this guard dog.

Thankfully my training kicked in, and I placed my briefcase between the dog and me with an outstretched arm. This confused the dog. He tried to go around the briefcase to get to me, but each time I would bring it around to face him, which stopped his advance. After a couple of these dance moves, he settled down between me and the access off this front porch and the safety of my car.

But once he got over his initial fear of the briefcase he kept slowly inching forward, baring his teeth and growling. The dog was still confused as to how to get around my shield and get to me. At one point he was so close, I could feel his breath on my hand that was gripping the briefcase for dear life.

About the time my arm was giving out holding up the one thing between me and this growling dog, he sat down. I slowly lowered my arm but kept the briefcase hanging in front of me. *Now he is settling down and this is my chance,* I thought.

I made a move toward the safety of my car, and the dog went back into attack mode. I froze and put the briefcase back up, and this went on for what seemed like an eternity.

Finally, two hours into my ordeal, a highway patrol car came flying up the driveway with lights flashing and pulled up to the house. *I am ready for jail. Take me, Officer.*

The officer stepped out of his patrol car, whistled, and that mean killing machine that kept me trapped on the porch turned into a loving little puppy. I put two and two together and asked, "Is this your home, Officer?"

"Well yes, it is, son. I'm Officer Dan, and I see you have met Honey Cup," he said, grinning broadly.

Apparently, a neighbor had called Officer Dan and told him someone was trying to break into his home, and his dog had stopped him. Once the officer arrived on the scene, he realized that I was a door-to-door salesman and decided to have a little fun.

He called me over to his patrol car to be introduced to Honey Cup. My instinct was to make a run for it while I had a chance. But I forced a smile, sucked it up, and walked over to meet and pat the vicious animal's head. After I obeyed what I took as his order, he advised me that it was time to move on. I hightailed it out of there.

Despite what I had just gone through, I was determined to continue working that day and drove down the road to another house that I had a lead card on. I walked up and knocked on the door, and a little old lady came out. I introduced myself and told her why I was there.

She looked me up and down, and asked, "Are you all right, son?"

I figured I might still look a little dazed from the encounter with the guard dog. I said, "I'm okay, but what do you mean?"

"You look like someone who just lived through an encounter with Honey Cup," she said.

My jaw hit the ground, and I thought, *How does she know about what just happened?*

About that time Officer Dan drove up in the driveway, stepped out of his car, and yelled out, "Mom, why don't you make Doug and me a cup of coffee?"

Turns out he had called his mom and was telling her what had just happened at his house when I walked up on her porch and knocked on her door. The three of us had a great many laughs at my expense, but she ended up buying a policy from me and has referred quite a few new clients since then. Officer Dan became a good friend who always enjoyed relating this embarrassing story all over town. But I never saw Honey Cup again, and hope I never do.

The grapevine can produce some sweet results

In an earlier chapter I told you about how Betty appointed herself my eyes and ears in the tiny town of Ekalaka, Montana. While this was certainly a unique customer relationship, it does occur more often than you think.

I had made an appointment in Miles City, Montana, and made the three-hour drive to see a woman by the name of Alice. I had never met her before. She was a referral from another client. When I arrived at her home no one came to the door, but I heard a female voice call out, "Let yourself in. I am back here."

The door was unlocked, so I did as I was told. I didn't see anyone, but she called out again, "I'm in the bathroom. I need help."

To my shock, I found that my prospect had fallen in the bathtub and, due to her girth and her age, couldn't manage to get up. "Can you please help me?" she asked. "I've been here for three hours, and I was praying you'd get here soon."

I grabbed a towel and covered her with it and then hoisted her to her feet and out of the tub. "You are my hero, Doug!" she exclaimed.

I am sure I was beet-red, but after I got Alice standing upright we did a quick check to see if anything was broken. After confirming that she was okay Alice told me to wait in the kitchen while she got dressed, and she never mentioned it again. At least not to me.

She bought a policy that day, and she gave me the names of several of her friends who she thought might also be interested.

Each time I'd call on them, they'd invariably ask, "Now how did you meet Alice?"

I'd give some generic answer, and then I'd hear laughter on the phone or when I'd first meet with them face-to-face. I soon discovered Alice had explained to her friends how I'd rescued her without sparing any of the details.

Through Alice's referrals, I signed up half the women in that town.

> **"If you work just for money, you'll never make it. But if you love what you are doing and put the customer first, success will be yours."**
>
> **– Ray Kroc**

Put time and effort into your relationships

While I learned how to sell with my first company, I learned how to build relationships with my second. Forming a bond with clients takes time and effort, but sometimes by chance being in the right place at the right time can elevate you to hero status. Having clients like these two ladies and many others just like them made my career.

Without ongoing client relationships such as these, a salesperson wakes up every morning unemployed and spends 90% of their time trying to find a client to talk to. That gets hard to do day after day, and can be ten times more expensive than keeping an existing customer happy.

> **"Salespeople today are the differentiator. That's why it's so critical for you to focus on becoming a valuable business asset to your customers."**
>
> **– Jill Konrath**

Be a giver

Make yourself an integral part of whatever community you are in. Find causes that genuinely matter to you, but that also connect with a broad number of you clients. When you give of yourself, you help build confidence in those around you that you are about more than just money and just selling them something.

I love history. When we moved to this little town in east Texas, I joined the Historical Foundation, which had many members who were older longtime residents and knew everyone in the area. Not only did I get the great satisfaction of helping preserve this historical town, but I got a chance to work hand in hand with some great veterans and listen to their tall tales of the past. Plus, word spread quickly through town what I did for a living and how I could help those in need.

Everywhere I have worked, I've offered to do free speaking engagements on the updates or changes to government rules and regulations that affected the products that we offer to our senior clients. I typically present a free, 30-minute Medicare 101 seminar to local churches, senior centers, chambers of commerce, assisted living, and retirement homes. If asked, I provide business cards. I make sure we all have fun during this short session and that everyone leaves that seminar with new information.

Even if most never personally have a need for my products or services, it establishes me as the Medicare expert in my market. I still get calls from people who heard one of my seminars years ago and remembered who to call when they needed key information or some help with their Medicare.

On my outgoing emails, under my signature, for many years I've used this tag line as a reminder:

"You will get all you want in life if you help enough other people get what they want."

– Zig Ziglar

Knock-Knock Moments

- Demonstrate genuine concern for your client.
- Being sincere can help salvage a relationship.
- Make sure the grapevine is helping spread the word about your integrity and kindness.
- Figure out how you can best contribute to your community, and devote yourself to those causes.

The Close:
A Revolution in Sales

*"Approach each customer with the idea of helping
him or her solve a problem or achieve a goal—not of
selling a product or service."*

– Brian Tracy

Across the board, no matter what you are selling, I'm guessing that there have been big changes in your industry. During the five decades that I've been in insurance sales I've seen tremendous changes throughout the entire sales process, from distribution channels to how we communicate with our prospects and customers.

Although the majority of lessons I've shared with you in this book are time-tested principles that hold true today, any salesperson worth their salt knows that they must be prepared to make changes according to shifts in the market and rapidly changing technologies.

In fact, we had just gotten started on the book you are holding when the 2020 pandemic hit. Our primary target for our Medicare supplemental policies is people ages 65+—the very audience in the highest risk group for the COVID-19 virus. Within the first few months virtually all nursing homes/assisted living facilities put their residents on lockdown, and the rest of the seniors across the county were asked to go home and ride this pandemic out.

That presented a particular challenge for us for a few reasons. One, our products can be complicated and often require a lot of handholding with clients. Two, because our industry is highly regulated, we are not allowed to solicit for new business the way we used to. We would often get new clients by getting permission to sit in a lounge at a healthcare facility, at large retail events, county fairs or senior centers, and let the consumers approach us. Three, a good amount of our older clients are not tech-savvy during the best of times, so using technology to reach them likely wouldn't be as successful as we'd like. In fact, it's not uncommon to discover that some of them are still using flip phones.

As one of the more experienced senior executives in the U.S. in the senior healthcare marketplace, I was part of a fantastic organization that held many, many online meetings and Zoom calls where we discussed how to adjust to this new reality. We shifted gears and canceled two bi-annual in-person training conferences in Utah. And in less than two weeks, we rounded out a project to provide the bulk of that same training to our thousands of salespeople available virtually.

We quickly put together some specialized online training that helped teach our agents how to safely contact, educate, and service our key audience on the products they still needed when this pandemic hit. This quick adjustment not only allowed us to continue to provide our product and services, but our production went up more than 12% during this period.

All of this turmoil and uncertainty took place in the midst of a nationwide shortage of people trained to sell Medicare health plans, prescription drug plans, and life insurance Most of these products have been provided by independent agents who work from their homes and go visit with prospects and clients where they reside and show what plans are available in that market, which is referred to as the independent agent distribution channel.

Simultaneously, the insurance call centers, or direct sales channels, have been throttled by legislation to protect consumers from unwanted calls. This slowdown in direct channels has created a huge vacuum nationwide for someone to sell and service these type of products to the multitude of needy consumers.

Independent agencies have a historic opportunity over the next few years to get out in the marketplace, raise their hand, and say, 'Hey, we're here, and we have multiple choices for you." But the majority of existing independent agents and agencies are about to age out of this industry. We do not have enough new blood taking up this career opportunity fast enough under the current onboarding process to fill the gaps being left by the large carriers cutting back on their captive agent channels.

The vast majority of agents and agencies servicing this industry are over 65 years of age and are either retiring, dying off, or they have been doing this for years, are set financially, and no longer need or want to work. But in the senior market more than 11,000 people are turning 65 every day in the United States, and each one of them has their hand raised and is asking for some help in making the transition from their existing health plans into the world of Medicare. They need help with what steps to take, when they need to take these steps, and they need help in choosing the right Medigap, Prescription Drug Plan, or Supplement to help enhance their Medicare or Medicaid programs.

Over the next few years, we have more customers needing our help than we will have agents hired and trained to help them. What other industry can say they have this type of problem today?

Although our industry may be the extreme as an example of the dearth of trained salespeople available, I can make the argument that there is a lack of professional salespeople for some of the same reasons that not enough people are going into the trades. Apprenticeships have all but died. Sales as a profession rarely comes up as part of the conversation with the younger generations. It's not presented as an option in most schools.

I hope that our ride-along has opened your mind to the extraordinary possibilities a career in sales brings, and the multiple ways improving your sales skills can boost your career. I never dreamed when I answered that blind ad all those years ago what a fun ride I was about to take. My professional career in sales has brought Shirley and me a fantastic living, and a dream life filled with unexpected adventures that allowed me to meet wonderful colorful characters, help meet the needs of these customers, and make some life-long friends along the way. What else can you ask for in a career?

If I could leave you with just one piece of advice, it would be this: No matter what career path you take, live a good, ethical, and honorable life while doing it. Then, when you get older and think back, you'll enjoy it a second time.

Acknowledgements

While some names and identifying characteristics have been changed in the interest of privacy, some others have been proudly put into print as a thank-you for playing your part in building my career in sales.

The book you are holding and the stories you are reading were created by my experiences with thousands of people who allowed me to enter into their lives. Some knew I was coming but some just looked up and there I was. You are too numerous to mention individually, but too important to not mention at all.

Thanks to the multitude of motivational speakers, authors, and positive friends who helped keep my glass half full every day.

A special thanks to my late friend, Zig Ziglar, who had a huge impact on my career time and time again.

Thanks to Bryan Flanagan for offering to parachute in every time I needed a true motivational speaker.

Thanks a million, Mom and Dad, for giving me a great start. I miss you both.

And to Ron Kellogg, a friend for more than 40 years. Thanks for talking me out of retiring. I'm having a blast recruiting and training agents once again. Wish you were here.

Thanks to Echo Montgomery Garrett for convincing me to move forward with writing this book and then having the patience to teach this ol' dog the writing process.

About the Authors

Doug Thompson said in the first chapter that he never met a single soul who dreamed of being a salesperson. Doug didn't have that dream either, but he was born to be a salesman. Before finding his calling, he worked in oil fields and as a ranch hand in Montana. He tried his hand at truck driving, manufacturing oil field equipment, construction work in Texas, and spent two years building the London Bridge in Lake Havasu, Arizona. Answering a blind newspaper ad for a "sports-minded individual" put him on this path. After asking to ride along with one of the company's salesmen, he came back to the interview and said, "If he can do this, I can." And he has ever since.

Doug resides with his wife Shirley in Jefferson, Texas, where they purchased and restored a historic home dating to 1872 and transformed the carriage houses into a bed-and-breakfast. The couple originally moved to Jefferson with retirement in mind. But thoughts of retirement didn't last long for Doug. His passion for improving the customer's experience as well as the sales profession continues to drive him as he comes up with new ideas to answer this question: *How can we make the sales process better?*

Starting out as an insurance agent going down the street knocking on doors selling accident insurance, Doug quickly moved into the management side of the life and health insurance industry, hiring and training agents to be successful doing the same. Within a short period of time, his ability to build successful sale teams caught the eye of the corporate leadership of several major companies. Doug became the vice president of sales and marketing for Conseco, and was recruited to do the same for Pacificare, UnitedHealthcare, American Republic, Tranzact, and Humana.

Currently, he is the marketing director for a large national insurance wholesaler that recruits and trains insurance agents and agencies across the county, as well as continuing to build his own general agency, which offers life and health products to the senior population. He is known nationally for his innovations in the sales industry, and frequently speaks and trains on his favorite topic of sales.

Doug and Shirley have four children, nine grandchildren, and three great-grandkids so far. Doug is contemplating putting his earring back in.

If you are interested in becoming an insurance agent or owning your own agency drop Doug a note at Doug@Thompsoninsmktg.com

Journalist Echo Montgomery Garrett is the author of 21 books, including the multi-award winning *My Orange Duffel Bag: A Journey to Radical Change*. In 2013, it won the American Society of Journalists & Authors *Arlene Eisenberg Writing that Makes a Difference Award*, which is presented every three years to the book that's made the biggest difference in society. She was named *Georgia Author of the Year* in 2013 by the National League of American Pen Women. Her articles have appeared in more than 100 media outlets, including *AARP, American Way, Money, Success*, and *Inc*. She co-founded the Orange Duffel Bag Initiative, a 501c3 nonprofit that provides certified life-plan coaching and ongoing advocacy to young people ages 14-24 who are experiencing homelessness, poverty, or aging out of foster care. Echo resides with her husband Kevin in Marietta, Georgia.

Index

A

accountability, 26–27, 31
Adams, Patch, 21
Adkins, David. *See* Sinbad (David Adkins)
administrative details, 43
adversity, 65
affirmations, 58
Ash, Mary Kay, 61
assumed close, 73
athletics, 5–6
attitude
    adjustment, viii
    negative, 60
    positive mental, 57–65
    and success, 91
audience, knowing your, 77, 116

B

bad days, how to handle, 59
Baker, Montana, 1–3, 39
Banker's Life, 40
basics, don't forget the basics, 71
Billings, Montana, 39
blowback, 57
brand, personal, 109–118
    changing, 116
    check-up, 116–118
    determining, 118
    fits your mission and values, 116
    questions about, 110
Buck, Dave, 111
business card, 51, 54, 124
Butte, Montana, 64
buyer's remorse, 105

C

call to action, 52
car, first, 4
career progression, 35
centers of influence, 35
change
    adapting to, 127–129
    in industry, 127
    is constant, 116
    or die, 74
    world is not ready for, 6
childhood, 1–2
churn and burn, 36–38, 112
closing, 72–73, 97, 100
    ratio, 44
clothing. *See* Dress code
clothing store sales job, 39–40
cold calls, 10, 18, 37, 44, 59, 68–70, 82, 95
college, 5–7
Columbo technique, 50
commission, 10–11, 13, 21, 27
communication, 53
    non-verbal, 53
    reviewing, 59
    skills and success, 91
    style of prospect, 102
community, being a part of, 124–125
competitive spirit, 15–16, 18
complaints, dealing with, 98–107
concern
    addressing clients' concerns, 82–83
    for client, genuine, 122–123, 125
confidence, 53–54, 59, 68, 124
connections

building on, 37–38, 40
  genuine, 37, 41
conversation, starting, viii
Coolidge, Calvin, 13
couple, addressing a, 83–84
COVID-19. *See* Pandemic
cows, 3–4
Crisco, 6

D
deal killer, 101
decision-makers, 83–85, 89, 101
desperation, 23
details count, 54
Disney, Walt, 1
dominance position, 103
dress code, 29, 53
dressing
  the part, 52–54
  for your audience, 53, 101
dry cleaner, 46
Dunnel (Doug's Funnel), 44

E
Edison, Thomas A., 91
educator, 79
effort and success, 91
Ekalaka, Montana, 105, 122
elevator speech, 51–52, 56
email, 53–54, 116
enthusiasm, 68
Epictetus, 82
ethics, 130
etiquette in each situation, 80
examples in everyone, 74, 113
experience, 102
  ten years *vs.* one year ten times,
    67–68, 74
  using client's experience to imagine
    an accident, 82
expertise, sharing, 77–80
extra mile, 100

F
face-to-face meetings, 70
failure, 15
Falk, Peter, 50

familiarity and contempt, 45–47
family, 1–2, 11, 39, 58
feedback, 52, 68, 77, 116
flexibility, 83, 91–93
Ford, Henry, 49
Foreman, George, 15
Forsyth, Montana, 98
Fort Wayne, 38
funnel
  filling, 43–44
  resistance to, 44–45
  sorting hot prospects, 47
  visual, 44

G
game, winning by staying in it, 19
gas station/mini-mart/bait shop job, 8
gender, 83–85
German shepherd, 120–122
Gitomer, Jeffrey, 68
giver, being a, 56, 124
giving up, achieving victory by not giving
  up, 19
goals, 28–29, 33
  approaching client to help achieve, 127
  constant thinking about, 30
  daily review, 32–33
  lifestyle goal, 30–32
  Mount Everest goals, 30, 32
  needs goal, 30–31
  reasons for, 28
  SMART goals, 30
  writing down, 29, 32
Godin, Seth, 68
grapevine, 122–123, 125
gratitude, viii
growth, importance of, 67

H
Hartman, Jason, 110
head in the game, 59–61
Hill, Napoleon, 29
history, 124
home
  observing, 85–86
  office, 53

Honey Cup, 120–122
horse, 3–4
hot button topics to avoid, 86, 101, 104
Howard, Vernon, 74
humility, 63–64
humor, 28, 114–116, 118
hunger, need for, 60

I
Iacocca, Lee, 81
icebreaker, viii
importance, making people feel they
     have, 61
impression, first, 52–54, 56
     bad, 101
independent agent distribution channel,
     128
Indianapolis, 36, 38
industrial engineering, 5–6
industries, looking to other, 70, 74
insurance
     license, 11, 14
     license school, 14–15
integrity, 125
intuition, 102–103, 107

J
job
     determining if it is right for you, 12
     learn from each job experience, 12
     vs career, 35–41
judgment, snap, 62–64

K
Kimball, Spence W., 78
kindness, 107, 122–123, 125
K-Mart, 36
knee injury, 5–6
knock-knock joke, viii
Knock-Knock Moments, 12, 19, 24, 33,
     41, 47, 56, 65, 74, 80, 107, 118,
     125
knowledge, 68
     generosity with, 76–80
know what you want, 21
Konrath, Jill, 123
Kroc, Ray, 123

L
Lake Havasu, 7
leads, 45, 69, 107
     bad, 44
     employer-generated, 49–50, 68
     generation, 50
     from networking, 55
     third-party, 44
     third-party, buying, 44
learning, importance of, 67–74
LinkedIn, 53–54
listening, 81–82, 101
     active, 83
     instead of thinking about what to say
          next, 82
     and respect, 83–84
     skills, developing, 89
Lombardi, Vince, 25
London Bridge, 7–8
love what you do, 123
Lufkin Industries, 8
Lugar, Richard, 36–37
lunch, invitation to from prospect, 76

M
magic, 97, 100
management, 7, 72
     style, 38
manners, 93–95, 100
marketing
     churn-and-burn approach, 112
     doing your own, 49
     techniques, traditional, 49–50
marriage, 11
McAuliffe, Christa, 75
McCulloch, John, 7
Medicare supplemental health policies,
     60, 69, 105, 124, 127–129
mental attitude, positive, 18
mentoring, 68
Midenhall, Jonathan, 101
Miles City, Montana, 122
Minot State, 5–6
Monday meetings, 16, 18, 23, 26–27, 71
Montana State University at Bozeman, 6
motel housekeeper, 8

motivation, 18, 28, 45
    and goals, 29
    photograph, 29–30
Muncie, 38

N
namedropping, 35
naysayers, 19, 57, 65
negative thoughts, strategies
    for deleting, 65
networking, 55–57
    choosing groups, 55–56
    family and friends, 56
Nightingale, Earl, 58
numbers. *See also* Scorecards
    and accountability, 26–27
    as a barometer, 28
    story from, 25–26, 33
    tracking, 25–26

O
observation, power of, 84–85
oil field, 4–5, 7
Oklahoma, 2
Olivier, Sir Laurence, 35
online calls, 53
online training, 128
openness to learning, 73–74
opinion, time in which one is formed, 52
opportunities, don't miss, 56, 68–70, 100
opposition, turning into ally, 98–107
options, keeping them open, 12

P
pandemic, 70, 127–128
payment, 96–97
pen, carrying a, 54
persistence, 13, 95–97
personality style of prospect, 103
photographs, 29–30
pride, sidelining, 71–73
problem-solving approach, 127
product knowledge and success, 91, 101
prospecting, 43–44
    amount of time spent, 49
    everyone is a prospect, 35, 47
    family and friends, 45–47

first impressions, 101
as funneling process, 44
genuine ways to connect while,
    37–38, 41
golden rules of, 43–47
Googling, 54
from home, 53
hunting for, 39
personal observation, 47
Prospect or Die, 45
prospect's communication
    and personality style, 103
prospects of your own *vs.*
    third-party, 44
research prospects, 54
sorting hot prospects, 47
taking names, 54
talking about aspects of your
    products/services, 104
waiting for prospect to come
    to you, 50

Q
questions
    about products/services, 104
    and hot buttons, 104
    open-ended, 103–104, 107

R
ranch hand, 2–3
rattlesnakes, 3
reading, 58
recommendations, 51
referrals, 27, 122–123
    and Medicare supplemental insur-
        ance, 70–71
    from satisfied clients, 120
rejection, 23, 57, 64
relationships, 40–41. *See also* Connec-
    tions, building on
    building, 119
    building, signs of success, 120
    personal, 119
    put time and effort into, 123
    salvaging, 120
reminders, positive, 58

respect, 83–84, 89
ride along, viii, 10, 16, 68, 87, 101
Rogers, Will, 67
Roosevelt, Theodore. *See also* Connections, building on
rules, unspoken, 76, 80

S
Safeway, 9
sales
  appetite for, 45
  basic sales skills, 13
  continued focus for success, 22
  educating yourself about, 68
  finding the right approach, 41
  genuine, 120–121
  negative attitude towards, vii
  percent of time spent selling, 43
  reframe as a profession, viii
  as self-employment, 22
  studying the product, 13
sales call
  steering wheel review, 26, 33
Salesforce.com, 27
salespeople, need for in insurance
  industry, 129
sales record, 18
scarcity and desirability, 98–100
schedule
  discipline, 24
  prioritizing, 23–24
schedule correlates with income, 22
school visit, 77–79
Schwan Home Service, 69
score, keeping, 25, 33
scorecard, 43
scorecard motivation, 19, 26–27
scorecards, 30–33
secret agent, 61
selling
  people don't like being sold,
    110–111
  people like to buy from those they
    know and trust, 110
selling where you are, 64
selling yourself, 50

sell where you are, 50
seminars, 124
Shell Oil, 1
shortcuts, 22–23
shotgun, 112
signs, reading, 76
Sinbad (David Adkins), 117
sincerity, 125
situations, approach with open mind and
  heart, 80
sleeping on the job, 87–89
social media, 53–54
software tracking systems, 27
speaking, public, 114–115
steering wheel review, 26, 33
Stein, Ben, 119
stereotype of sales person, 57
Stone, W. Clement, 57–58
strengths, identifying, 113–116
study skills, 14
success, vii, 18, 22–23, 25, 28–29, 38,
  43, 57–58, 95, 112–113, 119–120,
  123, 128
  sustainable, 91

T
talk about what you do, 45–47, 50–51
talking, too much talking and missing
  information, 82, 89
Tannen, Deborah, 85
teaching moments, 75–80
TedTalks, 68
Texas, 2, 8
Thompson, Shirley (wife), 8–9, 11, 40,
  58, 95, 115
time
  management, 21–23
  as a valuable asset, 24
timeliness, 101
Tracy, Brian, 30, 43, 68, 127
truck driving, 39
truthfulness, 111–113
trying, continue, 91

U
union work, 7

V

values, being true to, 116–118
Vaynerchuck, Gary, 109
vehicle, 54
video calls, 53
view, taking the long view, 12

W

webinars, 68
women
    as decision makers, 84–85
    in sales, 85
wrong *vs.* uncomfortable, 38–39

Y

YouTube, 68

Z

Ziglar, Zig, vii, 33, 58, 64, 67, 93,
    95, 124
Zoom, 70, 128